Authentic Apocrypha

The Dead Sea Scrolls &
Christian Origins Library
2

Authentic Apocrypha

False and Genuine Christian Apocrypha

by

James H. Charlesworth

BIBAL Press

North Richland Hills, Texas

BIBAL Press
An imprint of D. & F. Scott Publishing, Inc.
P.O. Box 821653
N. Richland Hills, TX 76182

Copyright © 1998 by J. H. Charlesworth
All rights reserved.

Printed in the United States of America

02 01 00 99 98   5 4 3 2 1

Library of Congress Cataloging-in-Publication Data
Charlesworth, James H.
    Authentic Apocrypha : false and genuine Christian Apocrypha
/ by James H. Charlesworth.
        p. c m. -- (The Dead Sea scrolls & Christian origins library
: 2)
    Includes bibliographical references.
    ISBN 0-941037-63-0 (pbk. : alk. paper)
    1. Apocryphal books (New Testament) I. Title. II. Series.
    BS2840.C48 1998   97-53301
    229'.92--dc21   CIP

Dedicated to and in honor of
Mario Erbetta, Helmut Koester,
Luigi Moraldi, James M. Robinson,
and Wilhelm Schneemelcher

Excerpts from the Authentic Apocryphon
Titled the Gospel of Thomas
(In my translation, parentheses denote words added for meaningful English.)

Jesus said, *"If those who gather you should say to you,*
'Behold, the Kingdom is in heaven,'
then the birds of heaven will precede you.
If they should say, 'It is in the sea,'
then the fish will precede you.
But, the Kingdom is within you and it is without you.
When you know yourselves,
then you will be known
and you will understand that
you are the sons of the Living Father.
But if you do not know yourselves,
then you are in poverty,
and you are poverty."
(Logion 3)

The disciples asked Jesus,
"Tell us what the Kingdom of Heaven is like?"
He said to them:
"It is like a mustard seed, which is smaller than all seeds.
But when it falls on the tilled soil,
it produces a large branch,
and becomes shelter for the birds of heaven."
(Logion 20)

Jesus said,
"Love your brother as your (own) soul;
Protect him as the pupil of your eye."
(Logion 25)

Contents

Preface

    Authentic Apocrypha is the title chosen for this collection to placard the fact that the Apocrypha and Pseudepigrapha of the New Testament are genuine early Christian compositions. Far too often, scholars jettison the early Christian apocryphal compositions from the study of Christian origins. New Testament experts ignore them because they are not in the canon. This is an unsophisticated approach, since the decision to include only twenty-seven writings within a category called the "New Testament" postdates the origins of Christianity by centuries. Patristic experts do not study them because they are not part of "Patristic Literature." Experts on Gnosticism tend to dismiss them because they are not clearly "gnostic" and were not found in the "gnostic library" near Nag Hammadi.

    The title is chosen to shock scholars and others out of unexamined presuppositions. The New Testament Apocrypha and Pseudepigrapha (NTAP) contain the gospels, acts, epistles, and apocalypses that were considered genuine by many Christians from at least the second century until well after the canon was summarized by Athanasius in the late fourth century. If you were to ask Christians in Rome, Jerusalem, Alexandria, Athens, Antioch, and Edessa in the third century what they knew about Jesus the Christ, they would tell a story at once familiar and full of unknown details. They also would begin his biography by describing how Joachim and Anna brought their daughter, Mary, to the Temple to fulfill their promise, much like Hannah did for her son, Samuel, at the house of the Lord at Shiloh. Mary lived from the ages of three to twelve in the Temple, when she was given to Joseph who was divinely chosen to be her husband. These Christians would quote sayings of Jesus not found in the canonical gospels; for example, this one:

> He who seeks will not rest until he finds.
> And he who has found shall marvel.
> And he who has marveled shall reign.
> And he who has reigned shall rest.

The early Christians would tell a story unknown even to most scholars today. They would continue to tell how Jesus was crucified between Titus, on his right, and Dumachus, on his left. They would relate that Titus entered paradise before Jesus, because he protected Mary, Joseph, and Jesus (when he was a child) when they passed through the wilderness infested with robbers. They would continue a story rich with details, until they described how Jesus shouted from the cross, "my Power, my Power, you have forsaken me!" Then they would animatedly recount how Jesus was raised by God. They might conclude by telling how Peter was crucified upside down in Rome and Paul was beheaded in the same city. These early records are preserved respectively in the *Protevangelium of James*, the *Gospel of the Hebrews*, the *Arabic Infancy Gospel*, the *Acts of Peter*, and the *Acts of Paul*.

These early writings are "authentic" in the sense that many of the Patristics and early Church scholars thought they were genuine. These documents, dating from the second and third centuries, are to be categorically distinguished from the "false" apocrypha, like the *Letter of Lentulus*, which is a medieval attempt to create something like one of the authentic apocrypha of the Church.

Today, scholars are divided about the importance of the Christian apocrypha. All agree that they are essential for understanding the early history of the Church, but virtually none are assigned as readings in introductions to early church history. Some experts on the historical

Jesus, like Crossan, conclude that the NTAP are invaluable in reconstructing the life and teachings of Jesus. Others, like Meier, judge that they are worthless in Jesus research. I am convinced that the truth lies between such extremes.

Some apocrypha are still lost. For example, in a lost Solomonic apocryphon we are told, according to *Paul's Epistle to Titus*, that Solomon stated, "They perform abortions in secret, but at the same time think they will live for ever."

This monograph is issued with the hope that more people (both scholars and non-specialists) will turn to the NTAP and enjoy what many early Christians considered "gospel truth." It is inconsistent of New Testament specialists to relegate the NTAP to the status of discarded books because they are shaped by legends and myths, and then at the same time revere Matthew's use of legends and myths in his Infancy Gospel. We should all admit that much of early Christian literature is shaped by myths, but that these myths are the best way we humans have for conveying to others our most precious truths and feelings.

As this monograph moves through BIBAL Press I wish to thank Dr. Bill Scott for his excellent work on it. I am grateful to Princeton Theological Seminary for research grants and for the permission to publish, in a revised and fuller version, some work that appeared in The Princeton Seminary Bulletin. I am also grateful to Walter de Gruyter of Berlin and New York for permission to republish, in a significantly revised form, my "Research on the New Testament Apocrypha and Pseudepigrapha," which appeared in 1988 in *Aufstieg und Niedergang der Römischen Welt* (II.25.5). The remainder of this monograph is published for the first time.

JHC
Princeton
December 23, 1997

Abbreviations

Altslavischen Apok	Santeros Otero, A. de. *Die handschriftliche Überlieferung der altaslavischen Apokryphen*, 2 vols.
ANF	The Ante-Nicene Fathers
ATLA	American Theological Libraries Association
BA	*Biblical Archaeologist*
BCE	Before Common Era (= BC)
BHT	Beiträge zur historischen Theologie
CE	Common Era (= AD)
Cod. Apoc. NT	Fabricus, J. *Codex Apocryphus Novi Testamenti*, 2 vols.
DBSup	*Dictionnaire de la Bible, Supplément*
ET	English translation(s)
GAL	Bardenhewer, O. *Geschichte der altkirchirchen Literatur*, 4 vols.
GosTh	*Gospel of Thomas*
HeyJ	*Heythrop Journal*
JBC	*The Jerome Biblical Commentary*
JTS	*Journal of Theological Studies*
LCL	Loeb Classical Library
NovT	*Novum Testamentum*
NT	New Testament
NTAP	New Testament Apocrypha and Pseudepigrapha
NTS	*New Testament Studies*
OT	Old Testament
OTP	Old Testament Pseudepigrapha
RHR	*Revue de l'histoire des religions*
TLZ	*Theologische Literaturzeitung*
TU	Texte und Untersuchungen
WUNT	Wissenschaftliche Untersuchungen zum Neuen Testament
ZPEB	*The Zondervan Pictorial Encyclopedia of the Bible*, 5 vols.

Introduction

The old man sat down. He crossed his legs and began to write on a fresh sheet of papyrus. He was tired, having spent all day with his students. He allowed himself a brief moment of pride in what he was accomplishing. He was heralded as one of the leading scholars in one of the intellectual centers of his world, but he knew that he would not walk the paths of this Earth much longer. He longed for sleep, but he was driven by an irresistible compulsion, by a conviction that there was a task God wanted him to complete. He must record for posterity the important truths that burned within his heart and which he had heard from his teachers. Sighing, he looked at the sheet, which glowed dimly in the flickering candle-light. *I wonder,* he thought, *if someday in the distant future someone like me will look at this sheet and think about the man who put words to it. Ah, but enough of this idle fantasy; there is work to be done. . .*

This man exists only in my imagination. Ocassionally, I think of such a scribe as I bend over an ancient manuscript and touch parchment, papyrus, or leather that preserves words nearly two thousand years old. I wonder what the copying scribe was like. I can often tell something about his motivation, just by reading his words, but in some mystical way I intermittently feel his presence. I long to know more about his dreams, his daily life, his character. How old are the traditions he preserved for us?

The works of a very few of these ancient scribes found their way into Scripture. They are part of what we call the canon, the list of approved works that form our Bible. Obviously, most of the ancient religious writings never became scripture and probably—like some of the writings in the New Testament—were never intended as such.

There is a third group of writings. These were written by people who were just as dedicated and convinced of the truth of their words as were the writers of our scriptures. Many of these works were considered to be scripture (or nearly so) among the communities in which they first appeared. Yet, over time they were discarded. Their adherents were too often declared to be heretics, or for some other reason a consensus never developed that they were apostolic and belonged in the canon.

We have two terms to describe works that are not part of the canon. One is *apocrypha*, Greek for "something hidden." Sometimes the term is used to refer to works which must be "hidden" from the uninitiated because of their esoteric nature. Other times, the term is used as an insult, to describe something that is unworthy of the light of day.

We even know of religious communities which regarded as apocryphal some works which are considered canonical today. For instance, the books of the "intertestamental period" which the Roman Catholic Church regards as "deuterocanonical"—added to the canon—are considered apocryphal (non-canonical) by Protestants, even though they may be included in bound editions of the Bible from the fourth century to the present.

The second term is *pseudepigrapha*. This term refers to sacred writings of Jews and Christians, composed generally from about 200 BCE to 425 CE. Many of these works were considered "canonical" or at least were highly respected within numerous communities, but for reasons we cannot yet discern, they were never accepted by the larger religious community. Some of these works were copied and kept in the libraries of monasteries. Others were buried under the rubble of ancient churches or synagogues that were destroyed or abandoned as their members died out or were driven into other lands.

In modern times, archaeological discoveries and intensified biblical studies have brought to light some of these long buried works, and have renewed interest in the study of others which were not lost, but were largely forgotten. As popular interest in these "hidden" books has grown, scholars often also have to deal with the task of identifying forgeries and works that are not what they claim to be. Many of these false works are quite old and fascinating in their own right, as they cast light not on Christian origins, but on the medieval world. "Authentic Apocyrpha" are the documents that date from the early centuries of the Common Era.

1 The Letter of Lentulus

An Obvious Fake

A few years ago a well-meaning person read the *Letter of Lentulus* to a group of religious people in Miami, Florida. The impression was given that the document contained a somewhat reliable description of Jesus' physical appearance. A reporter called my office in Princeton, he assumed that the "letter" was authentic or at least ancient. Was it an another example of the sensational writings from the first century coming to us from caves in the desert east of Jerusalem? Was it like the letters of Bar Cosiba which have been found in desert caves, or like the letters found among the Dead Sea Scrolls? Is it not conceivable that this "letter" provides a reliable portrait of Jesus?

Obviously many people during this last decade of the second millennium are becoming confused by the often spectacular and challenging archaeological discoveries.[1] It is imperative to stress at the outset that the *Letter of Lentulus* is not one of the new discoveries. It was well known in both academic and lay circles one hundred years ago.

The entry on "Jesus Christ" in the 1871 edition of *Smith's Dictionary of the Bible* concludes by quoting this document.[2] The document, often called "a pen portrait of Jesus," is attributed to a certain Publius Lentulus, presumably a contemporary of Pontius Pilate. He allegedly wrote the letter to the Roman Senate during the reign of Tiberius Caesar (14–37 CE). Here is my translation:[3]

A certain Lentulus, a Roman, who was an official for the Romans in the province of Judea, during the time of Tiberius Caesar, and who saw Christ and noted his mighty works, preaching, innumerable miracles, and other stupendous deeds, wrote to the Roman senate the following:

In this time there appeared a man, who lives till now, a man endowed with great powers, named Jesus Christ. He is called a prophet of truth by the Gentiles; his own disciples consider him the Son of God. He restores the dead to life and cures the sick of all manner of diseases. This man is of moderate height and worth seeing, with a venerable countenance, so that those who look at him both love and fear him. His hair is the color of a prematurely plucked hazelnut, and smooth almost to the ears, but from the ears in encircling curls, a little more glossy and shining, flowing over his shoulders, and divided down the center of his head after the fashion of the Nazarenes. His forehead is even and very serene; and his face, without wrinkle or blemish, is enhanced by a ruby color. Nose and mouth are in no way faulty. His beard is full, of the same color as his hair and not long but parted in the middle. His appearance is simple and mature. His eyes are diverse hues of azure blue and exceedingly brilliant. In reproof he is terrible; but in admonition he is gentle and amiable, joyous yet dignified. Sometimes he weeps, but never laughs. In stature of body he is developed and erect;[4] his hands and arms are beautiful to see. In speaking he is deliberate, serious, and modest. He merits what the prophet said: his handsomeness surpasses the children of men.

Obviously, readers of this book will not be duped into thinking that this portrait of Jesus is accurate and genuine. Nevertheless, let us begin with a focused question: Is it not conceivable that the *Letter of Lentulus* provides a description of Jesus of Nazareth that was written by a Roman official while Jesus was alive?

In the past, the answer to the question by many was frequently an unqualified—and uncritical—"yes." During the last century and the early decades of this century the *Letter of Lentulus* was customarily read as a reliable description of Jesus of Nazareth. It even appeared in family Bibles and in popular works.

Scholars have known for over 500 years that the so-called *Letter of Lentulus* is fictitious and have attempted to demonstrate this judgment to the masses. In the year 1440, Lorenzo Valla (c. 1406–57), the humanist highly esteemed by Martin Luther and many others, became famous for proving that the *Donation of Constantine* was a fake (*De falso Credita et Ementita Constantini Donatione Declamatio*). He examined the alleged letter while he was under the protection of King Alfonso I of Naples. This precursor of modern historical criticism claimed that the so-called *Lentulus Letter* was spurious.[5]

In his monumental *Dictionnaire des Apocryphes* of 1858 M. L'Abbe Migne warned that the "Lettre de Publius Lentulus" was a fabrication of the thirteenth or fourteenth century.[6] In 1867 B. Harris Cowper in *The Apocryphal Gospels* judged this work to be "a late mediaeval [sic] forgery."[7] *The Cyclopedia of Biblical, Theological, and Ecclesiastical Literature* of 1867–1887 informs the reader that the fictitious letter "carries within itself the proofs of its spuriousness."[8] In the 1871 edition of *Smith's Dictionary of the Bible*, the reader may be impressed by the way the article on "Jesus Christ" concludes, but miss the judgment that the work is "not authentic." In 1924, Montague Rhodes James, who held prestigious and distinguished academic positions such as Provost of Eton and Provost of King's College, Cambridge, advised in *The Apocryphal New Testament* that this *Letter* "can hardly be earlier than the thirteenth century: probably it was written in Italy."[9]

The consensus among scholars is unequivocally clear. The *Letter of Lentulus* has nothing to do with the historical Jesus or with the origins of Christianity; it was composed during the late Middle Ages.[10] The work is neither included nor even mentioned in the recent collection of the New Testament Apocrypha and Pseudepigrapha by W. Schneemelcher which was edited and translated into English by R. McL. Wilson.[11] In the Italian collections of the Christian apocryphal works it is rightly branded as a thirteenth or fourteenth-century forgery by M. Erbetta and L. Moraldi.[12] In his work titled *Modern Apocrypha* E. J. Goodspeed in 1931 pointed out that the *Letter of Lentulus* is merely "a fiction, designed to give currency to the description contained in the painters' manuals about the personal appearance of Jesus." He dated it "probably as old as the thirteenth century."[13] In his *Strange Tales About Jesus* Per Beskow assigns the *Letter* to the world of medieval compositions in perhaps the thirteenth century.[14] In J. K. Elliott's revised edition of James's *The Apocryphal New Testament* a translation of the *Letter of Lentulus* based on E. von Dobschutz's edition of the Latin appears with the succinct yet lucid statement that we are reading a "thirteenth-century text" which is "in the form of a letter purporting to have been written by a Roman official, Lentulus, at the time of Tiberias Caesar."[15]

The opinions of scholars is impressively consistent and without qualification; but, such individuals as those in the Miami church have a right to ask, "Why is the work spurious?" Why is the *Letter of Lentulus* a medieval forgery? There are numerous good reasons for this conclusion.

First, the texts are considerably diverse and very late; the original language is apparently Latin but translations exist in German, French, Italian, Spanish, English, Syriac,[16] Persian, and Armenian manuscripts.[17] No text, including the Latin, antedates the fourteenth century; and that means that we have no evidence that the work was available before that date. We do have compositions of other works, like the *Books of Enoch* and the *Testament of the Twelve Patriarchs*, that are preserved in late medieval manuscripts, but most of them now appear in early fragments of manuscripts or are quoted by the early scholars in our culture (Jews, Christians, and sometimes so-called pagans). Thus, neither do we have an early fragment, nor do we have an early quotation from this work attributed to anyone in the family.

Second, the introductions are confused. The oldest one does not label the work a letter. In the earliest text, the *Letter* is not attributed to Publius Lentulus. In other introductions, he is hailed as having such fictitious titles as "President of Judea" or "President of the Jerusalemites" (*Hierosolymitanorum prases*).[18] The daughter versions apparently derive ultimately from the Latin, and they—especially the Syriac—tend imaginatively to embellish and improve Jesus' physical appearance.[19]

Third, this individual is never mentioned in antiquity; he never existed. No Roman during Jesus' time was ever called "President," and no Lentulus was ever prefectus or procurator of Judea. The pseudonymous "Lentulus" has no link with the famous Lentulus family, which was Roman and patrician. But, it is obvious why a medieval author would choose this well-known family for a pseudonymous composition. In the decade before 200 BCE. Lucius Cornelius Lentulus served under Scipio Africanus, the illustrious general who defeated Hannibal. Lentulus Clodianus fought against Sparticus, though not proudly, and then was one of Pompey's legates against the pirates. Publius Cornelius Lentulus Spinther was renowned for advocating the recall of Cicero from exile in 57 BCE. Gnaeus Cornelius Lentulus, proconsul of Asia, defeated the Getae who lived on the southern section of the Danube, was a close friend of the Emperor Tiberias, and left him considerable wealth. Gnaeus Cornelius Lentulus Gaetulicus was legate of Upper Germany during the ministry of Jesus and wrote poetry which inspired the Latin poet Martial (c. 40–101 CE).

Fourth, the person who fabricated the work was ignorant of pre-70 Palestine. The reference to Jesus' hair as the color of hazelnut, dark blond, and his eyes of azure blue depict not a Jewish male but an "Aryan Jesus."[20] Judaism is conspicuously absent in this account; perhaps the depictions of Jews with hooked noses during the Middle Ages alert us to a possible anti-Jewish sentiment in "Nose and mouth are in no way faulty." Yet, the lack of Jewishness and Jewish features in the *Letter* seem indicators that western culture is replacing the authentic Jewish Jesus with an Aryan Jesus.

Fifth, additional spurious claims abound in the letter. These cumulatively clearly prove that the document is a medieval forgery. It is unlikely that a Roman during the time of Jesus knew about the customs of the Nazarites, of whom the author's ignorance surfaces again, since he confused them with the Nazarenes. A Roman official during Jesus' time would certainly have written to the emperor who controlled the Levant and not to the Roman senate. A Roman would certainly not use Semitisms like "the children of men" (*filiis hominum*) which easily derive from the New Testament and not from some Semitic source.

Sixth, a Roman also would not cite a biblical prophet ("he merits what the prophet said," *ut merito secundum prophetam*). The scriptural text cited surely seems to be Psalm 45:2 ("You are the most handsome of men") which was not one of the early Christian testimonia thought to allude to Jesus. The appeal to or dependence on this psalm again indicates much later Christian apologetics. David, whom the author assumed wrote the Psalm, sometimes is considered to be a prophet.

Seventh, Jesus' physical appearance was unknown to the early scholars of the Church—a fact which would certainly be startling if his appearance had indeed been described to the Roman Senate. Eusebius and Augustine reported that nothing is known about Jesus' appearance. Centuries later, Luther speculated that he was not necessarily "handsome."[21] Admiring Jesus because he never laughed betrays the hand of some medieval monk, who was a Gentile, and obviously thought of Jesus as "one who is called a prophet of truth by the Gentiles" and as "the Son of God."

Eighth, unlike such writings as the *Letters of Christ and Abgarus,* the *Letters of Pilate and Herod,* and Paul's *Third Epistle to the Corinthians*—which derive from the early centuries of Christianity and belong within the corpus of the New Testament Apocrypha and Pseude-pigrapha[22]—the *Letter of Lentulus* itself appears for the first time around the thirteenth century and is not cited in the early centuries.

Ninth, the *Letter* provides nothing new. Every-thing it contains can be derived, with a little imagina-tion, from the Gospels of Matthew, Mark, Luke, and John. The report that Jesus was called "Jesus Christ," indicates a Christian author. Jesus was not known as the "Christ" when he was a Jewish male living in ancient Palestine. This title was given to him by his fol-lowers, after they believed God had resurrected him from the dead around 30 CE, and especially after the first century, when Christianity moved farther and far-ther away from Judaism.

Tenth, the description is idyllic. A Roman who did not believe in Jesus could not have written this pseu-donymous letter. It is substantially different from the core of Flavius Josephus's *Testimonium,* which is authentic and thus contains concepts and terms that are surprising and indeed inappropriate for a Christian.[23]

Eleventh, also indicative of a late date is the pro-Roman sentiment. This Publius Lentulus is associated with Tiberius Caesar. He admires—even adores—Jesus. This attitude reflects the shift away from history to romance. The letter was obviously written at a time when the admiration of Jesus by many of his Jewish contemporaries had been shifted in the popular Christian mind to the Romans, who were, in fact, guilty of his condemnation and crucifixion. In other words, the text assumes a post-fourth-century political environment in which the Romans have become those whom the Christians wish to win over, or are, in fact, members of the post-fourth-century Holy Roman Empire.

Twelfth, the pro-Roman sentiment of the *Letter of Lentulus* is similar to the "conversion" of Pilate imagined by later Christians. Despite his whitewashing in the later strata of the canonical gospels and demonstrably in the apocryphal works attributed to him,[24] he did condemn Jesus to be crucified, as virtually all historians have indicated. While Pseudo-Lentulus is medieval, Pilate was indeed the prefect of Judea when Jesus was crucified. An inscription bearing Pilate's name has been recovered in Caesarea on the coast of Israel. It dates from Pilate's time (26–36 CE) and it is now clear that he was a prefect and not a procurator.

Christian legends have misled not only the public but also devout Christians. History, for example, was rewritten so that Pilate worshipped Jesus. According to the fourth-century (or later) *Acts of Pilate* some Christians imagined that when Pilate saw Jesus he worshipped him. In the equally apocryphal and late *Revelation of Stephen*, Pilate accosts a crowd demanding Stephen's death, charging them that they had compelled him to crucify "the Innocent One." The words are attributed to Pilate who is referring back to Jesus; and he is using a Christological title.

Thirteenth, the pictorial *Letter of Lentulus* supplies a physical description of Jesus as an ideal and attractive man. That interest indicates that it was composed in the Middle Ages, probably sometime during or after the thirteenth century when so many images were created. Christians at that time requested such an account; virtually no Christian today requires such a description of Jesus' physical characteristics. Perhaps the *Letter of Lentulus* was fabricated to "authenticate" one of the numerous "portraits" of Jesus that appeared in the thirteenth century, the great age of forged art works.

Fourteenth, the different copies and versions of the *Letter* are not the same. It appears that the earliest copies did not contain the name "Lentulus" at all—only later was it known as the *Letter of Lentulus*. As best as we can determine, the earliest mention of the name "Lentulus" is in the manuscript now in Jena. This copy was reputedly found by the famous Roman family, Colonna, in Rome about the year 1421—just about nineteen years before Lorenza Valla suggested it was a fake.

Fifteenth, I am suspicious that the Colonna family, jostling for a more powerful political position, found a description of Jesus and attributed it to one of their famous ancestors—in the process baptizing a Roman as a Christian following a questionable reading of 1 Corinthians 15:29 (which refers to the custom of being baptized on behalf of the dead). The practice of improving one's standing through an enhanced genealogy was common in Italy in the thirteenth, fourteenth, and fifteenth centuries.[25] In any case, there seems no reason to doubt the conclusion of Dobschutz: this spurious work was produced in Italy in the thirteenth or fourteenth century.[26]

You may have heard all kinds of wild accusations that scholars, politicians, or religious leaders have suppressed publication of some of the Dead Sea Scrolls because they prove some religious beliefs to be false. In light of these and other scandalous charges against Christian belief being disseminated by self-serving "scholars" who misread and misunderstand the Dead Sea Scrolls—especially those which are not yet officially published—it is understandable why some people today feel moved by reading the *Letter of Lentulus*. They have been misled into thinking that the Dead Sea Scrolls have not been published because they have been hidden from the public by Christian scholastics. Perhaps, they imagine, the *Letter of Lentulus* is original, but hidden from the public by "eggheads who are hiding truths." These myths are perennial but fraudulent.

Scholars (and I do not use this term loosely to include teachers or "professors" who claim to be "scholars") have been serving the public well. These highly trained individuals have illustrated that such literary creations as the *Letter of Lentulus* were composed long after Jesus' time, and have historical value only in so far as they reveal medieval credulity and open up windows to glance into a false depiction of first-century culture by medieval speculators.

Is there absolutely no redeeming value in a pen portrait? In a certain sense, one can acknowledge that it is a monument to the love Christians have for the earthly Jesus. Christians need to be reminded that he was one of us. He suffered like each of us. Christians honor him as divine and call him "Lord"; and in worshipping him or through him they should not forget that he was a first-century devout Jewish male who was sentenced to death by the Prefect Pontius Pilate, and crucified by Roman soldiers outside the walls of Jerusalem during the Passover feast in 30 CE. Everyone has the freedom, and the right, to imagine what he may have looked like. Historically informed imaginations, however, need to be guided by some realities. Late medieval forgeries should not be confused with early Christian apocryphal compositions that were considered inspired and "canonical" by some Christians before there was an accepted and closed canon. Inauthentic apocrypha, like the *Letter of Lentulus*, should be separated categorically from true and authentic apocrypha, like the *Gospel of Thomas*. Only authentic apocrypha originate in the early centuries of the Common Era.

This gold coin was struck at Constantinople during the reign of Justinian II (705–711 CE). It shows Christ holding the Gospels in his left hand and raising his right hand in benediction. Justinian reportedly believed this to be an accurate representation of Jesus based on early portraits commissioned by Constantine I. Note the short, frizzy hair, beard, and long nose.

Of course, we have no reason to believe that Justinian knew any more about Jesus' appearance than we do, but it is evident that he knew nothing of the supposed description provided by Pseudo-Lentulus.

[Photo courtesty of Edward G. Waddell, Ltd., Greek, Roman, and Byzantine coins, 444 N. Frederick Ave., Suite 316, Gaithersburg, MD 20877, 301 990-7446.]

A tomb in the Kedron Valley that was most likely constructed in the first century BCE. Notice the evidence of Greek influence. According to the *Gospel of the Nazaraeans*, the man with a withered hand (Mt 12:9–14) was a mason who earned a living by constructing buildings. [Photo by James Charlesworth]

Joppa and the Mediterranean Sea. Joppa was the site of many early Christian apocryphal episodes, especially regarding Peter; these were usually based on Acts 9–11. [Photo by James Charlesworth]

Bethzatha (John 5) and the remains of the alleged Asclepian Shrine. Asclepius, the god of healing, was one of the most prominent dieties at the beginning of Christianity. Christianity inherited from this religion and so was able to eventually dominate it. [Photo by James Charlesworth]

Roman forum. Apocryphal tradition has Paul imprisoned not far from where this picture was taken. [Photo by James Charlesworth]

2 The English Editions of the New Testament Apocryphal Works

These reflections on the spurious nature of the *Letter of Lentulus* bring up an obvious question. Where can one find out if a work actually belongs among New Testament Apocrypha or Pseudepigrapha? In order to answer this question, we must first agree on a definition of the term, New Testament Apocrypha and Pseudepigrapha (NTAP). The NTAP is a modern collection of writings that were composed before the end of the fourth century, when there was not yet an accepted definition of orthodoxy, heresy, or canon, and that were usually written in imitation of the documents eventually considered canonical.[27] Like the collection of writings in the New Testament, the NTAP contains letters (or epistles), gospels, acts, and apocalypses.[28]

Fortunately, now is an opportune time to assess what is available. I shall focus on three major publications that have appeared recently: *Ancient Christian Gospels* (1990), *New Testament Apocrypha* (1992), and *The Apocryphal New Testament* (1993).

Ancient Christian Gospels (1990).[29]

The John H. Morison Professor of New Testament Studies and the Winn Professor of Ecclesiastical History at Harvard Divinity School, H. Koester, is famous for his insistence that Christian origins must not be reconstructed with only, or primarily, the intracanonical

writings in mind. He has argued since the early sixties
that some so-called apocryphal writings are early and
independent of the New Testament works. For
Koester, for example, the *Gospel of Thomas* is not dependent on the intracanonical gospels. It often preserves sayings of Jesus as early and as reliable as the
Synoptics[30] and John.

In *Ancient Christian Gospels: Their History and Development*, Koester argues persuasively that the *Gospel of
Thomas* was composed in eastern Syria (p. 80). In con-
trast to R. M. Grant and E. Haenchen who brand it
heretical and reject it as a second-century fabrication,
Koester contends that *the tradition* of Jesus' sayings in
the *Gospel of Thomas* predates the intracanonical gospels (p. 85). The author of this work "was certainly not
trying to compose a 'gospel' of the type that is known
from the Gospels of the New Testament" (p. 80), and
the sequence of sayings is "most puzzling" (p. 81).

In light of the tendency among many scholars to
view the *Gospel of Thomas* only with an eye on the Synoptics, Koester shows that it is also a very important
aid in interpreting the Gospel of John.[31] He correctly
shows that in certain passages *Thomas* and John preserve early traditions about Jesus which each developed, often in strikingly different ways.

One of the many important aspects of Koester's
work is his demonstration that the word "gospel"
(*euangelion*) originally did not describe a certain type
of writing. Instead, "gospel" referred to the message
of salvation as a whole (1 Thess 3:6, 1 Cor 1:17,
15:1–15, cf. Acts 15:7, 20:24). Koester shows that the
titles of the "gospels" became set only in the late second century (a claim that will be debated by experts,
notably M. Hengel),[32] and that none of the Nag

Hammadi "gospels" were designated by their authors as gospels.

Thus Koester's book begins with an examination of the development of "gospel" from oral preaching, through "memoirs of the apostles," to a literary genre. After examining the collections of Jesus Sayings (in Paul and the post-apostolic writings, *Gospel of Thomas*, and Q[33]), he traces the development of gospel dialogues from the *Dialogue of the Savior* through collections of miracle stories to the Gospel of John. He then studies the Synoptic Gospels in light of such compositions as the *Secret Gospel of Mark* and the *Proto-Gospel of James*. He concludes by exploring the origin of the gospel harmonies which do not appear for the first time with Tatian (who composed the Diatessaron[34] in Syriac probably around 175 CE) but can be traced back through Justin Martyr to harmonizations in Matthew and Luke.

Particularly appealing is Koester's full view of Christian origins, the recognition that we must be sensitive of the ways many early Christians revered writings that western culture eventually rejected or ignored, a perception of the significance of Eastern Christianity, and the appreciation of Thomas and his importance in the development of Christianity. Some of these same insights are developed in my own book, *The Beloved Disciple: Whose Witness Validates the Gospel of John?*[35]

New Testament Apocrypha (1992).[36]

After the fervent interest in early sources and the intermittent excitement with the discovery of such treasures as Codex Sinaiticus,[37] Syrus Sinaiticus,[38] the

Didache,[39] and the *Oxyrhynchus Papyri*,[40] a need was felt for a handy edition of the New Testament Apocrypha. A scholarly yet convenient collection of translations was required. This was supplied by Edgar Hennecke, a pastor in Betheln (Hanover), in 1904, and a subsequent edition was edited by Wilhelm Schneemelcher of Bonn University and translated into English by R. McL. Wilson of the University of St. Andrews in Scotland. In 1989, the fifth edition of volume two and in 1990 the sixth edition of volume one appeared in German. It was edited by Schneemelcher alone, since Hennecke had passed away in 1951.

These volumes were edited and translated into English by R. McL. Wilson under the title *New Testament Apocrypha*. The first volume contains the so-called apocryphal gospels and related writings. It also presents a general introduction which discusses the time in which these apocryphal works were composed and the processes—sociological and theological—that led to a closed canon. Of considerable interest to pastors and lay persons will be not only the discussions of unknown and lost gospels, but also of "gospels" attributed to Jesus' disciples and people linked with him according to the intracanonical gospels, notably introductions and translations (but not texts) of the following (in the order of their appearance in the volume):

> *The "Secret Gospel" of Mark*
> *The Gospel of Thomas*
> *The Gospel of Philip*
> *The Gospel of Peter*
> *The Gospel of the Twelve Apostles*
> *The Gospel of the Seventy*
> *The Gospel According to Matthias*

The Gospel of Judas
The Gospel of Bartholomew
The Gospel of Mary
The Protevangelium of James
The Gospel of Nicodemus
The Gospel of Pseudo-Matthew
The Gospel of Gamaliel

Sections on the infancy and on the passion of Jesus, as well as on the relatives of Jesus are full of data important for an understanding of Christian Origins.

The second volume of the *New Testament Apocrypha* presents introductions and translations of documents attributed to the apostles, apocalypses, and related subjects. The volume also contains a reliable introduction, including a section on the "apostle" in early Christian tradition. Acts attributed to Jesus' apostles are the following:

The Acts of Andrew
The Acts of John
The Acts of Paul
The Acts of Peter
The Acts of Thomas
The Acts of Peter and the Twelve Apostles

The second volume also contains a study of apocalypticism in Early Christianity and notably apocalypses attributed to Peter, Paul, and Thomas. Wisely included are the Christian sections of the *Ascension of Isaiah*, the *Fifth and Sixth Books of Ezra*, the *Sibyllines*, and the *Book of Elchasai*. Well over one dozen European New Testament and Early Church History experts have contributed to these volumes.

The impression should not be given that the English-speaking reader is given only an English translation of a German translation of a document, which itself may be a translation of a lost original. R. McL. Wilson informs the reader that while the English is based on the German introductions, the German translations of the apocryphal works have been checked with "the Latin, Greek or Coptic" (vol. 1, "Preface to the English Edition")—he should have included Syriac (e.g., see vol. 2, p. 409, note 155).

The Apocryphal New Testament (1993).[41]

Long before Hennecke and Schneemelcher's two-volume work was first translated into English by R. McL. Wilson in 1962–1965, the need was felt in the English-speaking world for a translation into English of the major apocryphal works. This was supplied in 1924 with the handy volume of translations by M. R. James, Provost of Eton and "Sometime Provost of King's College, Cambridge." It was titled *The Apocryphal New Testament*.[42] Now this work is updated in a volume about the same width but an inch taller by J. K. Elliott, senior lecturer in theology and religious studies at the University of Leeds. It is not as extensive as the *New Testament Apocrypha*, and sometimes perpetuates some of James's errors;[43] but it is intermittently more up-to-date and a direct English translation of the ancient texts.

The modern collections of the "non-canonical" gospels, epistles, and apocalypses present in attractive format documents that were written in the early centuries of this era (circa second to fifth centuries) and were once considered authoritative and inspired within numerous Christian circles. In some communities, several were accepted as part of the New Testament canon, and many were read with the understanding that they were full of God's revelation. As well as the so-called Patristics (the Apostolic Fathers), the New Testament Apocrypha and Pseudepigrapha are simply indispensable documents for perceiving and reconstructing the origins of Christianity and its sacred texts.

Unfortunately the word "apocrypha" connotes that which is spurious or inauthentic; and, hence, some Christians avoid the writings as if they would be contaminated by reading them. The *Letter of Lentulus* is surely fictitious and a fake; the writings in the New Testament Apocrypha and Pseudepigrapha should not be so branded. These writings, on the one hand, should not be considered "scriptural" in a theological sense, but they *were* considered scriptural by some early Christians and are as important for understanding the early centuries as some of the writings of the early scholars of the Church (like Ignatius, Justin, Irenaeus, Origen, and Eusebius). They also are essential in discerning the developments in the transmission of Jesus' sayings, and do contain insights for helping us reconstruct what Jesus intended to teach.[44] It is a pity that the NTAP do not receive the attention they deserve in theological and academic circles and in theological and university curricular offerings.

What is most surprising about the new editions of *The New Testament Apocrypha* and the *Apocryphal New Testament*? It is the incorporation of the so-called *Secret Gospel of Mark*. An introduction and translation of this work appears in each collection, but it may well be just as spurious and late as the *Letter of Lentulus*. It was allegedly found in 1958, but searches for the document have all ended in failure. Yet, H. Merkel judges that it probably dates "not before the middle of the 2nd century,"[45] which would mean it was perhaps composed sometime between 150 and 200. Elliott includes the work, but rightly warns that "its antiquity and genuineness are questioned by scholars."[46] The reader needs to be warned that some specialists today think that the so-called *Secret Gospel of Mark* may be a fabrication created in the seventeenth century or even more recently. Only when scholars have examined the copy of this document can we be closer to the truth (I have discovered that the work was moved from a monastery in the Judean desert to the library of the Greek Orthodox Church in Old Jerusalem, but even there, working with the new librarian, I have not been able to locate it).

Perhaps a section concerning documents not to be considered among the NTAP would be a helpful addition in future editions of the two major collections.[47] Likewise, many works listed in *The New Testament Apocrypha and Pseudepigrapha* are not even mentioned in any of the recent collections. It is disappointing also to observe that none of the recent collections of the NTAP offer the reader a translation of the earliest Christian hymnbook, which is attributed to Solomon.[48] It was included in earlier editions of E. Hennecke's and W. Schneemelcher's collection by the distinguished expert W. Bauer,[49] but was relegated to an appendix in the English translation of 1965. R. McL. Wilson justified the omission of the *Odes of Solomon* because the volumes needed to be reduced in size and the *Odes* were available in other editions.[50]

The *Odes of Solomon* are poetic compositions that are full of beautiful theological insights. They are worth reading for numerous reasons, including devotionals—some graduates of Duke University and Princeton have based sermons on them. Note, for example, the following beautiful passage:

> As the wind moves through the harp
> And the strings speak,
> So the Spirit of the Lord speaks through my
>   members,
> And I speak through his Love. (*Ode* 6:1–2)

Also appealing is the *Hymn of the Pearl*, which is judged to be "splendid" by Elliott (p. 441) and "one of the most beautiful products of Syriac literature" by Han J.W. Drijvers in the *New Testament Apocrypha* (vol. 2, p. 330). More people today should hear such words as these:

> Awake, and rise from your sleep.
> Listen to the words in this letter,
> Remember you are the son of kings,
> You have fallen beneath the yoke of slavery.[51]

The importance of the apocryphal compositions is now also highlighted by D. M. Smith's suggestion that the Gospel of John may be labeled the "first apocryphal gospel" in the sense that it intermittently preserves Jesus traditions independent of the Synoptics, in a way similar to the apocryphal gospels.[52]

If one is looking for a full introduction with comments by an international team of experts, then the best collection of the early Christian apocryphal works is the *New Testament Apocrypha* ($35 and $42). If one prefers a more succinct collection with translations by an English scholar then the choice is *The Apocryphal New Testament* ($49.95).

Charlesworth (white shirt on the right) in the library of the Greek Orthodox Church in the Old City of Jerusalem, with the librarian and scholars, searching for the *Secet Gospel of Mark* and other apocryphal works. [Photo by James Charlesworth]

Countless artists have been inspired by the Pseudepigrapha, and one of their favorite subjects has been the ascension of Mary as in this work by the German artist Tizian.

Pompeii. Probably a demonic satyr. The *Acts of Andrew* begins with a demon recognizing Andrew and calling him "this god-fearing man." [Photo by James Charlesworth]

First-century storage room for wine at Bethsaida (Julia), the home of Andrew, Simon Peter, and Philip (John 1:44). [Photo by James Charlesworth]

A model of Herod's Temple constructed under the guidance of leading Israeli archaeologists. According to the *Protevangelium of James*, Mary, Jesus' Mother, was in the Temple, nurtured by doves and an angel, from the age of three to twelve, when she was given to Joseph, an old man. [Photo by James Charlesworth]

3

Research on the New Testament Apocrypha and Pseudepigrapha over the Years

In this chapter, I will summarize some of the research which has been published on this subject. Later, I will identify authentic apocrypha and pseudepigrapha of the New Testament, discuss their value for modern readers, and identify some of the other fakes.

Renewed Interest in the NTAP

In 1936, Walter Bauer developed an important argument that changed the nature of studies of the New Testament Apocrypha and Pseudepigrapha. He demonstrated that so-called "heresy" often was older than orthodoxy in many early Christian communities.[53] In addition, the scholarly focus on Christian origins caused by the recovery of the Dead Sea Scrolls and the Nag Hammadi Codices[54] in the late forties, helped create an unparalleled international interest in the NTAP. About the year 1965, we entered into a new phase of intensive interest in and research upon the NTAP. Scholarly research may be divided into four phases.

The first phase of interest in the NTAP began sometime during the Middle Ages when there was increased interest in the apocalypses and the Antichrist. Among the documents in the NTAP that were singled out for the most attention was the *Protevange-lium of James*, today renamed the *Birth of Mary*, accord-ing to the title in the Greek papyrus. Three major tendencies marked this phase: the assessment of the NTAP in light of the superiority of the canon, the pre-occupation with dogma, and (ironically) the judgment that many apocryphal writings are reliable and authentic. This first phase continued through the eighteenth century.[55]

The second phase basically encompasses the nineteenth century. The first two tendencies in phase one continued unchanged; but the rise of rationalism, the pervasive critique of traditions, and the search for knowledge according to the post-Enlightenment and post-Kantian mood caused a gradual collapse of the third tendency; hence faith in the reliability of apocry-phal writings declined. Almost all of them came to be regarded as false; some even as scandalously misin-formed and misleading. There were highs and lows during the nineteenth century, representing succes-sively the critique of the canonical gospels and dogma by F. C. Bauer and the Tübingen school in Germany, the effects of revolutions in 1848, the pervasive influ-ence of the great philosopher Hegel (and criticisms of him), and the expanding horizons and additional manuscripts obtained by France's conquests in the Near East and later by British conquests in the same area.[56]

The third phase began about the beginning of the twentieth century. The first tendency, seeing the NTAP in light of the superiority of the canon con-tinued; the second tendency, a preoccupation with dogma, waned markedly.[57] The third tendency, judging the apocryphal writings as authentic, passed completely into oblivion.

A new, fourth tendency emerged, reflected in the works of Resch, but now sparked to a new level of interest by the discovery of the Oxyrhynchus papyri. This tendency is a keen interest in the lost gospels and "forgotten" sayings of Jesus.[58] This interest in the agrapha, or lost sayings of Jesus, was made popular by many scholars, especially J. Jeremias in his *Unbekannte Jesusworte*.[59]

Beginning around 1965 there was a renewal of interest in the NTAP. The tendency to see these writings only in light of the superiority of the canon began to wane. This awakening freed them for appreciation on their own merits, as reflected in the *Introduction to the New Testament* by H. Koester.[60] It also helped remove the canonical straitjacket into which the NT writings had been forced, allowing sensitive scholars to judge, as L. Keck has argued,[61] that the New Testament really is not a separate field of study.

We have entered into a new era, characterized by a wider appreciation of Early Christian writings: Why should scholars feel apologetic about being interested in the apocryphal writings when their colleagues are content to read the apostolic fathers? Why should a historian, a biblical scholar, or a history-of-religions specialist treat one document differently than another, the *Didache* in a different manner from the *Odes of Solomon*, the Gospel of John from the *Gospel of Thomas*? The only possible answer is the confessional commitment to a closed canon. And this answer reveals a deep-seated bias that tends to impair the trustworthiness of our best work.

The first tendency has only begun to wane; and
we can report this advance by looking at the courses
offered by our best universities and by the interests of
distinguished colleagues throughout the world. The
second tendency, a preoccupation with dogma, has
ceased. The third tendency, judging the apocryphal
writings as authentic, has also concluded. The "new"
or fourth tendency—a search for lost sayings of
Jesus—continues and is a characteristic of some of the
most recent scholarly publications. In the United
States, Koester has been appealing to the early and
reliable nature of some of Jesus' sayings in the NTAP.
For many scholars, the search for the actual words of
Jesus now includes a more appreciative awareness of
the sayings of Jesus in the apocryphal documents.[62]

Putting exaggerations aside, I think one must now
admit that some of the gospels recovered during the
last one hundred years have been judged too harshly,
and only in the light thrown on them by the canon.
The so-called apocryphal writings have indeed been
shaped by later communities; however, nothing is
clearer from our recent research than the fact that the
Gospels of Matthew, Mark, Luke, and John have likewise been heavily redacted (composed and/or edited
in stages). None of them preserves an unedited
recording of Jesus' words. Redactions (editing) are
characteristic of our received traditions, whether they
are inside or outside the canon. Yet, I am convinced
that the search for Jesus' authentic words is not futile
and that the best research in this area of scholarship
will demonstrate that the search for Jesus' own
meaning must no longer be limited to the canonical
documents.[63]

The Series Apocryphorum of the Corpus Christianorum

In the late fall of 1983, an invitation from the Facultè de Thèologie of the Universitè de Lausanne enabled me to speak about my work on the NTAP with the specialists in Switzerland who are contributing to the "Series Apocryphorum" of the "Corpus Christianorum." A second, longer visit occured in July 1997. It is clear that they define the NTAP in a way appreciably different from the traditional manner represented, for example, by Fabricius, Minge, James, and Hennecke—Schneemelcher—Wilson. The traditional approach seeks to define the corpus of the NTAP in terms of the canonical New Testament, and also, of course, in terms of the other collections (like the Apocrypha and Pseudepigrapha of the Old Testament) which receive their definition or description primarily in relation with and reflections on the canon.

Preparing the works for the "Series Apocryphorum" is a team, which is called 'L'Association pour l'Étude de la Littérature Apocryphe Chrétienne (AELAC). This team intentionally avoids the term "New Testament" and calls the collection the "Christian Apocryphal Literature." Note the following official description of the project:

> This [the Series Apocryphorum] includes essentially what are usually called the New Testament apocrypha (the gospels, acts, epistles, apocalypses). But to relate these works only to the New Testament is to underestimate the variety of this literature. Its scope is wider: It embraces pseudepigraphs or anonymous

texts of Christian origin where the main subject is
characters named in the Bible or present at events
described in biblical texts. Texts such as the *Ascencion of
Isaiah* or the *Apocalypse of Zachariah* belong to this
literature insofar as they have become gradually
Christianized, although they concern characters of
the Old Testament and build on Jewish traditions.

The need to break with the classical definition of
NTAP and to collect all the Christian apocryphal literature into one series is defended by E. Junod in
"Apocryphes du NT ou Apocryphes Chrétiens Anci-
ens?" (*Études théologiques et religieuses* 3 [1983] 409–21).
Now for the first time in one series we will have texts,
translations, and reliable introductions to this literature. The first president of the association, F. Bovon,
describes the format for the series as follows:

> Each book will have a common style and layout, but
> the structure will be that of the Early Christian work,
> for—in view of the variety and the importance of the
> ancient versions—we intend to include a modern
> translation of the texts. Because of the complexity of
> the problems of introduction and interpretation,
> ample space will also be devoted to commentary and
> notes.[64]

Critical editions of these Christian Apocryphal Works
appear in the famous *Corpus Christianorum, Series Apocryphorum*. Introductions and translations in convenient paperbacks appear in the series titled
"Apocryphes: Collection de Proche des L'AELAC."
The following significant books have appeared in the
latter series:

1. *L'Évangile de Barthélemy*, by Jean-Daniel Kaestli, 1993.
2. *Ascension d'Isaïe*, by Enrico Norelli, 1993.
3. *Histoire du roi Abgar et de Jésus*, by Alain Desreumaux, with Andrew Palmer and Robert Beylot, 1993.
4. *Les Odes de Salomon*, by Marie-Joseph Pierre, with Jean-Marie Martin, 1994.
5. *L'Épître des Apôtres* and the *Testament de notre Seigneur*, by Jacques-Noël Pérès, 1994.
6. *Salomon et Saturne*, by Robert Faerber, with a preface by Jean-Claude Picard, 1995.
7. *Actes de l'apôtre André*, by Jean-Marc Prieur, 1995.
8. *Actes de l'Apôtre Philippe*, by Frédéric Amsler, François Bovon, and Bertrand Bouvier, 1996.

The traditional and the new approaches to the NTAP are not contradictory but complementary. Both exclude the Nag Hammadi Codices, because they are superbly handled in separate collections and series. Both see the need to move beyond the fourth century in search of apocryphal documents. The traditional approach has the advantage of collecting into one corpus literature similar to and derivative from the New Testament. The new approach has the advantage of bringing together in a series all Christian apocryphal literature. The former is more conducive for specialists in the New Testament and Christian Origins; the latter is more helpful for Patristic scholars and historians of the early Church.

Description of the NTAP

After these necessary preliminary reflections, and a rapid review of the history of research on the NTAP, it is appropriate to recall our definition of the NTAP. The NTAP is a modern collection of Christian extra-canonical writings dating from the early centuries, perhaps from around 100 to 425, or from the decades in which the latest writings in the New Testament were composed until one century after Christianity became the state religion of the Roman Empire and the New Testament was widely considered closed. Documents later than the fifth century are included only because of the early traditions they may preserve or because they are organically related to the early compositions in the NTAP. The major characteristic of the documents in the NTAP is that they purport to be apostolic and spiritually equal to the twenty-seven writings in the New Testament.

To call these documents "apocryphal" does not mean to discard them or label them as unorthodox or inauthentic. Many are not secondarily derivative from the New Testament scriptures. It is imperative to remember that most of the documents in the NTAP were composed before the development of the closed canon, were revered in many "orthodox" Christian communities, are frequently preserved imperfectly or in fragments, and contain beneath late redactions sacred early traditions.

W. Schneemelcher also warned that a "strict application" of his definition of the New Testament Apocrypha would reveal that "many of the writings assembled there [in the first and second editions of the present work] could not be considered New Testament Apocrypha [vol. 1, p. 27]. His definition is similar to the description offered in the present monograph. See his scholarly opinion that a definition "may perhaps" be offered as follows:

The New Testament Apocrypha are writings which have not been received into the cannon, but which by title and other statements lay claim to be in the same class with the writings of the cannon, and which from the point of view of Form Criticism further develop and mould the kinds of style created and received in the NT, whilst foreign elements certainly intrude (vol. 1, p.27).

A portion of a horde of silver Roman coins found near Bethlehem, and not yet published. They were most likely hidden during the Bar Kokhba rebellion (132–135 CE). Each coin bears the portrait of an emporer. Until the beginning of the fourth century, Christianity struggled against emporer worship, and many early Christians were martyred. [Photo by James Charlesworth]

Cross on the top of St. Catherine's Monastery in the Sinai. In the monastery's library, many of the original copies of the apocrypha are preserved. According to the *Acts of Peter* 37, Peter was crucified upside down so as to represent Adam who fell head-downward (38). This photo is also on the cover of this book. [Photo by James Charlesworth]

The Judean Wilderness. This is the scene of Jesus' temptation and the location from which some apocryphal books have been recovered. [Photo by James Charlesworth]

4

Documents Not Considered New Testament Apocrypha or Pseudepigrapha

In the this section, I have listed the publications on the New Testament Apocrypha and Pseudepigrapha that are major studies, collections, texts, and translations, or are about the apocrypha and the canon. I have excluded from the NTAP six types of documents.

Apostolic Fathers

An early group of documents is categorized as "the Apostolic Fathers." A convenient and reliable edition of the Greek and English was published by K. Lake (*The Apostolic Fathers with an English Translation*, 2 vols. LCL. Cambridge, Mass., London, 1912; repr. from 1914 through 1965). It contains the following:

(Vol 1)
1 Clement
2 Clement
Ignatius
Polycarp
Diduche (Teaching of the Apostles)
Epistle of Barnabas
(Vol. 2)
Shepherd of Hermas
Martyrdom of Polycarp
Epistle to Diognetus

Some collections of the NTAP include one or more of these documents. Of this group, three writings—the *Didache*, the *Epistle of Barnabas*, and the *Shepherd of Hermas*—can make an impressive claim to belong within the NTAP. The last two are included in Codex Sinaiticus, one of the oldest Greek manuscripts of the Bible.

The Nag Hammadi Codices

Also excluded are the tractates found in the Nag Hammadi Codices. Many of these have titles similar to, even at times identical with, documents in the NTAP; but these documents are correctly gathered together in one group, both because they were found together in an ancient hoard of documents and because almost all of them are gnostic, and hence distinguishable from most of the writings in the NTAP.[65] To be distinguished from similarly titled documents in the NTAP are the following Nag Hammadi tractates:

Apocryphon of James
Gospel of Truth
Apocryphon of John
Acts of Peter
Gospel of Philip
Book of Thomas the Contender
Gospel of the Egyptians
Apocalypse of Paul
First Apocalypse of James
Second Apocalypse of James
Acts of Peter and the Twelve Apostles Apocalypse of Peter
Letter of Peter to Philip
Gospel of Mary

To avoid confusing these documents with similarly titled ones in the NTAP, I have referred to them with
prefixed qualifying parentheses; hence, the (Nag
Hammadi) *Apocalypse of Paul* is clearly distinguishable
from the *Apocalypse of Paul*, a document in the NTAP.

The Old Testament Pseudepigrapha

Excluded from the NTAP are also writings now included in the OTP. Among the latter collection are
some writings that are clearly Christian in the final
and present form.[66] Worthy of special note are the
following:

Apocalypse of Sedrach
Greek Apocalypse of Ezra
Vision of Ezra
Questions of Ezra
Revelation of Ezra
Apocalypse of Elijah
Apocalypse of Daniel
Testaments of the Twelve Patriarchs
Testament of Isaac
Testament of Jacob
Testament of Adam
Martyrdom and Ascension of Isaiah
History of the Rechabites
Odes of Solomon

It is not always easy to explain why these documents
belong in the OTP and not in the NTAP. Four good
reasons may be offered:

- They are originally Jewish writings or are
  heavily influenced by Early Judaism.

- They are attributed to Old Testament individuals or groups.

- They are often related in form to writings in
  the Old Testament or OTP, or are derived
  from one of them, and thus belong to cycles of
  literature in the OTP.

- The custom among scholars has been to place
  them in the OTP; and here I must emphasize
  that these literary categories are really modern conventions for organizing texts.

Early Syriac Writings

Some early Syriac documents, besides those included
in the NTAP—for example, the *Acts of Thomas*—
should not be included in the NTAP. The main reason
for this decision is that they fail to contain the major
characteristic of a document in the NTAP; that is, they
do not claim to be apostolic and spiritually equal
to the New Testament writings. Excluded are the
following:

Extracts from Various Books Concerning
   Abgar the King and Addaeus the Apostle
The Teaching of Addaeus the Apostle
The Teachings of the Apostles

The titles of these works indicate that they should be
included in the NTAP; but even a cursory reading of
them should convince the attentive reader that they
are fundamentally dissimilar to the New Testament
writings. They are legends developed by the Christians at Edessa, reflecting their desire to have roots

going back to Addaeus, or Thaddaeus, "one of the seventy-two apostles" (Extracts 6), who—they say— was sent by the resurrected Jesus through the apostle Thomas to convert the citizens of Edessa. These writings are related to but categorically different from the *Letters of Christ and Abgarus*.[67]

Earliest Versions Of the New Testament

A. D. Nock, in his assessment of Hennecke's third edition, lamented that Tatian could have received more attention.[68] Certainly there are ancient and apocryphal traditions preserved in the earliest versions of the New Testament, especially in the Old Syriac Gospels (in particular the Syrus Sinaiticus) and the Old Latin, as I have discussed elsewhere;[69] however, to add Tatian's so-called Diatessaron or any of the versions to the NTAP would confuse the already loose consistency of this corpus of literature. The harmony was produced by Tatian; it is neither an apocryphon nor a pseudepigraphon.

These brief remarks accentuate the fact that the study of the NTAP must go hand in glove with the examination of other noncanonical, but not apocryphal, writings. At least five categories other than the NTAP must be consulted.

- The canon itself

- The Apostolic Fathers (Patristics)

- The early Syriac literature

- The Nag Hammadi codices (and the other gnostic works such as the *Pistis Sophia*)

- The early versions of the New Testament

Fakes

Obviously, modern forgeries should be excluded from the NTAP. Almost all of these fakes were completely unknown to me, as they are to most scholars, and were brought to my attention—as I now learn was also the case for Goodspeed[70]—by students and curious individuals. Unworthy of scholarly attention, they are merely noted here in passing. Unfortunately, more fabricators should have come forward, as did Signor Gino Gardella,[71] and admitted that they had concocted a fiction in order to generate publicity for some event or publication. Many of these forgeries were discussed by Goodspeed in his *Strange New Gospels* and are now similarly criticized by P. Beskow in *Strange Tales About Jesus*."[72]

Foremost among these spurious works is *The Archko Volume*, or the *Archeological Writings of the Sanhedrin and Talmuds of the Jews; These are the Official Documents Made in These Courts in the Days of Jesus Christ,* "Translated by Drs. McIntosh and Twyman" (Philadelphia, 1913). Mr. W. D. Mahan, who claims to have obtained this so-called volume from the Vatican, was, to be polite, a clever novelist; to be frank, he was "found guilty of falsehood and of plagiarism, and suspended from the ministry for one year" (Goodspeed, *Strange New Gospels*, p. 56). Professor

Goodspeed's judgment is fair: "The whole work is a weak, crude fancy, a jumble of high-sounding but meaningless words, and hardly worth serious criticism. It is difficult to see how it could have deceived anyone" (p. 48).

The work is in many prestigious libraries, and can easily confuse the curious. In the twenties, M. R. James, in *The Apocryphal New Testament* (Oxford, 1924; p. 90), had to label it "a ridiculous and disgusting American book." And in the seventies, R. L. Anderson, a professor at Brigham Young University, lamented that,

> [S]ome Bible believers accept the Archko documents so that the book is often stocked in religious bookstores and periodically quoted to church audiences as containing "factual accounts" of those who came in contact with the Lord.

Anderson, of course, labeled it "a modern forgery," noting that,

> [P]erversions of fact contaminate virtually every page of the book, so that anyone with basic knowledge of ancient history, can multiply Goodspeed's random samples of blunders it contains.[73]

Enough has been said about modern hoaxes;[74] attention should not be drawn to them. They belong in no way to the ancient documents in the NTAP.

Possible Candidates

Numerous documents have been brought to my attention recently—either new discoveries or writings which have not yet been sufficiently examined. Most of these date too late to be included in the NTAP. Those that might be candidates for inclusion are the following:

The Gospel of Judas [lost]. Though early, perhaps from the second century, it is customarily excluded because it is supposedly an example of "gnostic perversions" of the truth. Judas, alone of the apostles, acted rightly; he was inspired.[75]

Jesus Pseudepigraph. (See J.-P. Migne, Jésus-Christ. ["Écrits attribués ou relatifs à Jésus-Christ," *Dictionnaire* 2, cols. 365–400.)

Passion of Ananias. (See A. De Santos Otero, *Altslavischen Apok.*, vol. 1, pp. 138–139.)

Quaestiones Apostolorum. (See A. De Santos Otero, *Altslavischen Apok.*, vol. 1, p. 210.)

Didascalia Domini. (See A. De Santos Otero, *Altslavischen Apok.*, vol. 2, pp. 233–236.)

De Arbore Crucis. (See A. De Santos Otero, *Altslavischen Apok.*, vol. 2, pp. 129–147.)[76]

The Rebellion of the Angels.[77]

Gospel of Barnabas.[78]

Gospel of the Simonians. Lost; but mentioned in the Arabic preface to the Council of Nicea.[79]

Gospel of Thaddeus. Lost; but mentioned in the Decretum Gelasianum.[80]

The Eternal Gospel.[81]

The Life of St. Anna.[82]

The *Gospel of Apelles.* This document, attributed to the disciple of Marcion, is early, perhaps dating from the second century. Epiphanius (*Haer.* 44) quoted a saying of Jesus from it. The reasons to exclude it

from the NTAP are that it is gnostic and not
attributed to a figure in the New Testament.[83]

The Teaching of Peter.[84] Little is known of this document. It
is not to be confused with the *Preaching of Peter.* I
have listed publications on it under the Peter
cycle.[85] Perhaps it deserves to be included in the
NTAP.

The Dialogue Between Christ and the Devil. This document is
difficult to exclude from the NTAP. It is similar to
the Christian expansion of the *History of the
Rechabites.* It is early enough (III-V cent.); however,
it appears not to be an apocryphon (a writing
similar in literary form to the NT writings, e.g.,
gospels, acts, letters, apocalypses), but a homily
on humanity's fate, Christ's conquest of the devil,
and the end of the world based on the NT
accounts of the temptation and the transfigura-
tion.[86]

The Apocalypse of Philip.[87] This lost work, used perhaps by
the author of the Irish work titled *The Evernew
Tongue*[88] was probably not an apocalypse.

These observations may help set the stage for a long
overdue scholarly discussion of the contents of the
NTAP.[89] These brief comments should help clarify
that it is difficult to distinguish an apocryphon from a
legend or a homily, and this fact reveals that our study
of the history and thought of early Christianity must
be more carefully attuned to the NTAP. The list of
documents placed in the NTAP as a result of my research is much longer than in any published collection; yet, without a doubt, other documents also
should be considered for possible inclusion in the
NTAP. No less than 104 documents are included in my
The New Testament Apocrypha and Pseudepigrapha.

It is impossible to develop and explain a set of criteria that will establish definitively what documents should be included in the NTAP. The history of Christianity, and its canonical concerns, cover far too many centuries and territories to enable us to arrive at anything more than a reliable approximation of the contents of this corpus.

A pre-Christian bronze serpent which is wound around a staff. It is unpublished. Ancient Ophiolatry mixed with Christology by the second century CE, and the Ophites worshipped Christ as the Serpent (cf. John 3:14). Ophite ideas are found in numerous apocrypha, notably in the *Apocryphon of James*. The third act of the *Acts of Thomas* is about the powerful and cosmic serpent. [Photo by James Charlesworth]

5

Introductions to the NTAP

I have profited from far too many introductions to list them all now. Attention will be drawn to those that are most reliable and recent. The classical works are, of course, the volumes by Fabricius, Migne, James, and Hennecke-Schneemelcher-Wilson. É Amann published a thorough, erudite and reliable introduction; since it was published in 1928, it is now somewhat dated. H. T. Andrews and P. Bigaré published convenient up-to-date introductions. The best major introductions, with translations, are the multi-volume works by Erbetta and Moraldi.

Of singular significance is a recent publication by a master of the apocryphal writings, namely H. Koester. Unusually important for a study of the NTAP is his *Introduction to the New Testament*, 2 vols. (Hermeneia; Berlin, New York, Philadelphia, 1982; the German original appeared in 1980).[90] This introduction centers upon the New Testament, but many of the documents in the NTAP receive significant discussion. Koester clearly appreciates the apocryphal writings and does not see them only in light of the New Testament. How refreshing it is to read his following words:

> It seems quite unlikely that any of the apocryphal texts was written during the apostolic period, but some of these writings may have been composed as early as the end of first century CE and a very large number are products of the second century CE. The NT Apocrypha

are therefore sources for the history of early Christianity which are just as important as the NT writings.
They contain many traditions which can be traced
back to the time of the very origins of Christianity.
They provide us with a spectrum that is much more
colorful than that of the canonical writings and permit
insights into the manifold diversity of early Christian
piety and theology, in short, a perspective which the
polemical orientation of the canon of the NT often
obstructs or seeks to limit [vol. 2, p. 13].

Perhaps the first tendency of research on the
NTAP—the perception and judgment of the NTAP in
light of the superiority of the canon—has finally begun not only to wane but to disappear. If so, it will be
typical of only the best scholars for some time.

6

The Gospel of Peter and the Passion Narrative

In the preceding discussion, I have stressed not only the redactional nature of all the gospels, including both the intracanonical and extracanonical gospels, but also to the tendency of scholars to give priority to the intracanonical gospels. Now, I would like to isolate for examination one gospel, the *Gospel of Peter*, about which some distinguished scholars have recently published some sensational claims.

One century ago, shortly after the discovery of a large fragment of the *Gospel of Peter*,[91] widely differing assessments of its traditions were stressed. A. Harnack claimed that this gospel was independent of the intracanonical gospels.[92] T. Zahn replied that it was dependent on the canonical gospels.[93] New Testament scholars and Patristic experts seemed to have been overly influenced by Zahn's position. For at least twenty years, I was convinced that the *Gospel of Peter* was clearly late and derivative from the intracanonical gospels. Now, the *Gospel of Peter* is receiving a new look—and not only from me.

In 1982, R. Cameron contended that the *Gospel of Peter* was independent of the intracanonical gospels and may even antedate "the four gospels of the New Testament and may have served as a source for their respective authors."[94] In 1983, Koester claimed that parts of the *Gospel of Peter* are independent and old.[95] The most sensational claims are now made by J. D.

Crossan, who in 1985 argued that the *Gospel of Peter* is certainly redacted, reflecting at places dependence on the intracanonical gospels, but that it also preserves a very old tradition that is prior to and indeed utilized by the authors of the New Testament gospels. Note his words:

> The *Gospel of Peter* contains three units which are independent of the intracanonical gospels and where, indeed, the dependence is in the opposite direction. These three units formed a linked and self-consistent complex which I call the Passion-Resurrection Source and which was used by all four of our intracanonical gospels.[96]

The first of these "units" is the passage concerning the "Crucifixion and Deposition." According to Crossan, this unit runs from verses 1 through 22, minus verses 3 through 5a which are redactional by the author who formed the traditions into the Petrine pseudepigraphon.

My translation of verses 1 to 22 of this alleged independent, pre-Marcan source follows.[97]

The Gospel According To Peter

(Brackets enclose reconstructed portions of the text that is damaged or missing. Parentheses circumscribe words added by me for idiomatic English.)

I

(1) But o[f th]e Jews none washed his hands, neither (did) Herod nor [a]ny of [h]is judges. A[nd] as they did [not] wish to wash (them), Pilate rose (from his seat).

(2) And then Herod the king ordered that the Lord
      should [be ta]ken away, saying to them, "All that I
      have ordered you to do to him, do."

II

(5) For it is written in the Law: "The sun should not set
      on one that has been put to death." And he deliv-
      ered him to the people on the day before the
      unleavened bread, their feast.

III

(6) But taking the Lord, they shoved him, as they ran,
      and said, "Let us drag the Son of God by force
      now that we have power over him." (7) And they
      put around him a purple robe, and set him on the
      seat of judgment, saying, "Judge righteously, 0
      King of Israel." (8) And one of them brought a
      crown of thorns (and) put it on the Lord's head.
      (9) And others standing by spat on his face, and
      others slapped him on the cheeks, others stabbed
      him with a staff, and some scourged him, saying,
      "With such honor let us honor the Son of God."

IV

(10) And they brought two criminals and crucified the
      Lord between them. But he remained silent, as if
      having no pain. (11) And when they had set up
      the cross, they wrote (upon it): "This is the King
      of Israel." (12) And laying down his garments
      before him, they divided them among themselves,
      and cast the lot upon them. (13) But one of those
      criminals rebuked them, saying, "We suffer,
      because of the evils which we have done; but this
      (man), who has become the savior of men, what
      wrong has he done you?" (14) And being angry
      with him, they ordered that his legs should not be
      broken, so that he might die tormented.

V

(15) But (though) it was midday, a darkness covered all
      Judaea. And they (the Jews) became anxious and
      distressed lest the sun already (had set), since he
      (Jesus) was still alive. (For) it is written for them:
      "(The) sun should not (set) on one who has been
      put to death." (16) And one of them said, "Give
      him to drink poison with sour wine." And mixing
      it, they gave (it to him) to drink. (17) And they
      fulfilled all things and completed their sins on
      their head.(18) And many went about with lamps,
      thinking that it was night; (and some) fell. (19)
      And the Lord called out, saying, "my Power, (my)
      Power, you have forsaken me!" And having said
      (this) he was taken up.
(20) And at the same hour the veil of the Temple in Jeru-
      salem split in two.

VI

(21)And when they withdrew the nails from the wrists of
      the Lord, they laid him on the earth. And the
      whole earth shook, and there was great fear. (22)
      Then the sun shone, and it was found (to be) the
      ninth hour.

This passage is complex, and gives conflicting impres-
sions. The anti-Jewish tone fits better the time after
Mark than before him. The distance from the Jewish
world and religion, as reflected, for example in the
words "their feast" and "it is written for them," do not
fit into the early Palestinian Jesus Movement that
existed as a sect before Mark. Mark's christology is
highlighted by the elevation of the title "the Son of
God"; hence, it is difficult to dismiss the possibility
that the *Gospel of Peter* is here dependent on Mark
or one of the intercannonical gospels. Numerous

questions arise as I read this tradition. Why is it only implied that Pilate apparently had washed his hands, as in Matthew 27:24; or is this part of the *Gospel of Peter* that is lost? Why does the criminal in this account rebuke "the people" (v. 5) and not the other criminal as in Luke 23:40–41?

And most impressively, why is it recorded that this criminal's legs were not broken and not Jesus' as in John 19: 31–37? Surely, here, as Crossan states (p. 144), John looks more redacted than the *Gospel of Peter*. But, that observation does not necessarily mean that the tradition in the *Gospel of Peter* is pre-Johannine, or pre-Marcan. I am presently persuaded that the *Gospel of Peter* may be independent of John. If so, that would be highly significant for this authentic apocryphon.

The traditions in this excerpt from the *Gospel of Peter* are important. Any study of the transmission of the passion narrative should include an examination of them. I am not convinced that this section of the *Gospel of Peter* is older than Mark; but it surely does indicate how early and multifaceted were the early traditions regarding the passion narrative. They are far more complex, lively, and contradictory than most New Testament experts have assumed. A study of the *Gospel of Peter* opens our eyes to the transmission of the gospel tradition. That conclusion seems evident, but it is not yet clear how early we are looking into the origins of Christianity.

Samaria from Sebaste. According to the *Pseudo-Clementines*, the magician named Simon was a Samaritan from the village of Gittha. He occasionally claimed he was the Messiah, the "Standing One." According to this apocryphon, Simon engages Simon Peter, but his power is defeated. According to the *Acts of Peter*, Simon Peter breaks the Samaritan's power of sorcery in the Roman Forum. [Photo by James Charlesworth]

Conclusion

Several years ago a friend and leading expert on the Dead Sea Scrolls joked with a journalist about what had been found in the Qumran Library, the library that dates from the time of Jesus and was found in eleven caves just northwest of the Dead Sea. Tongue in cheek, he said a letter had been found which was certainly a love letter from Samson to Delilah. The reporter fell for the joke and printed an announcement. The news spread rapidly from Jerusalem to even Panama City, Florida.[98]

The reporter's ignorance was manifest. Samson probably could not write, and he did not communicate with Delilah through the mail (there was no mail service in Samson's time). Samson lived long before we have evidence that Israel had become a writing society. No love letter from Samson to Delilah has been found among the Dead Sea Scrolls, just as no Lentulus met Jesus and penned a portrait of him.

The New Testament Apocrypha and Pseudepigrapha contains gospels, letters, apocalypses, and other compositions that are essential reading for anyone interested in the search for the transmission of Jesus' sayings not found in the New Testament, for the emergence of Christianity out of Judaism and into Roman civilization, and for a better perception of the lives of Christians in the second, third, and fourth centuries; that is, before the establishment of the institutional church by Constantine in the early fourth century CE. The authentic apocrypha, however, do not provide us with any dramatic new information about Jesus himself, and all such claims should be greeted with great

suspicion by all who are interested in the crucial question: "How did Christianity originate?"

Notes

1   For example, as this monograph reached a final draft, the evening news featured sensational archaeological claims. These were reported in *Time* (May 29, 1995): "Secrets of the Lost Tomb." The feature article, bearing the same name and with color photographs, ran from pages 48 through 54.

2   H. B. Hackett with E. Abbot, eds., *Dr. William Smith's Dictionary of the Bible* (New York: Hurd and Houghton, 1871) vol. 2, pp. 1385–86. I follow the title on the title page; the spine has *Smith's Bible Dictionary*.

3   For the Latin see E. von Dobschutz, "Epistola Lentuli," *Christusbilder Untersuchungen zur Christlichen Legende* (TU N. F. 3; Leipzig: J. C. Hinrichs'sche Buchhandlung, 1899) pp. 308–30, see esp. p. 319. My translation is based on the family d Latin manuscripts which all date from the 15th century. The superscription is unique to this recension.

4   Latin = *in statura corporis propagatus et rectus*. This can be translated in various ways: "in stature of body developed (enlarged, extended) and erect (upright)." Earlier the author referred to Jesus as of medium (or mediocre) height (*statura procerus mediocris*).

5   L. Valla, *De falso credita et ementita constantini donatione declamatio*, ed. W. Schwahn (Leipzig: Teubner, 1928) p. 62, "*Non hoc dico, quia negem effigies illas esse apostolorum, utinamque tam vera esset epistola nomine Lentuli missa de effigie Christi, quae non minus improbe ementita est quam privilegium quod confutavimus, sed quia tabella illa a Silvestro non fuerit exhibita Constantino. In quo non sustineo animi mei admirationem continere. Disputabo enim aliquid de fabula Silvestri.*"

6   M. L' Abbe Migne, "Lentulus," *Dictionnaire des Apocryphes* (Paris: Ateliers Catholiques, 1858) vol. 2, cols. 453–56.

7   B. H. Cowper, *The Apocryphal Gospels and Other Documents Relating to the History of Christ* (London: William and Norgate, 1867 [2nd ed.]) p. lxxxiii.

8 J. McClintock and J. Strong, "Lentulus, Epistle of," *Cyclopedia of Biblical, Theological, and Ecclesiastical Literature* (Grand Rapids, Michigan: Baker Book House, 1981 [reprint of 1867–87 work]) vol. 5, pp. 348–50.

9 M. R. James, *The Apocryphal New Testament* (Oxford: At the Clarendon, 1924) p. 477.

10 For bibliographical help see Charlesworth with J. Mueller, *The New Testament Apocrypha and Pseudepigrapha: A Guide to Publications, with Excursuses on Apocalypses* (Metuchen, N. J. and London: Scarecrow Press, 1987) pp. 248–49.

11 Schneemelcher, W., ed., *New Testament Apocrypha*, 2 vols., translation by R. McL. Wilson (Cambridge: James Clarke; Louisville: Westminster/John Knox Press, 1991-1992).

12 M. Erbetta, ed., "La Lettera di Lentulo," *Gli apocrifi del Nuovo Testamento* (Turin: Marietta, 1969) vol. 3, pp. 137–38. L. Moraldi, *Apocrifi del Nuovo Testamento (Turin: Unione Tipografico-Editrice Torinese*, 1971) vol. 2, pp. 1651–56.

13 E. J. Goodspeed, *Modern Apocrypha* (Boston: Beacon, 1931) p. 91.

14 P. Beskow, *Strange Tales About Jesus: A Survey of Unfamiliar Gospels* (Philadelphia: Fortress, 1983) pp. 3, 111–12.

15 J. K. Elliott, "The Letter of Lentulus," *The Apocryphal New Testament* (Oxford: At the Clarendon, 1993) pp. 542–43.

16 Syriac is a dialect of Aramaic—actually two, since there are Eastern and Western dialects of Syriac. The grammar and vocabulary are Aramaic, but the system for writing the characters of the alphabet differs from that of other Aramaic dialects. As the liturgical language of Eastern Christianity, this language has preserved a great number of ancient texts.

17 See S. P. Brock, "A Syriac Version of the Letters of Lentulus and Pilate," *Orientalia Christiana Periodica* 35 (1969) 45–62.

18 *"Leretulli praesidis in partibus Judaeae epistola ad senatores Romae de homine magnae virtutis nomine Christus."* See Dobschutz, *Christusbilder,* p. 317*.

19 The Syriac reads "the Jews consider him a prophet" for the Latin reference to Gentiles considering him a prophet of truth. If we were working with an ancient apocryphon, I would assume the Syriac has the earlier reading and that growing Anti-Judaism in Christianity, along with a Gentile bias, would give rise to the variant so that Gentiles and not Jews recognize Jesus' greatness. Also, the Syriac contains the color of Jesus' hair: "the color is dark red (*wswmq gwn' hw*)"; and this is a description that does not easily serve the Aryan myth of a blue eyed and blond Jesus who was by no means a Jew.

20 Elliott, following James, chooses the adjective "grey" to render the Latin oculis glaucis variis so that Pseudo-Lentulus refers to Jesus' grey eyes. Erbetta correctly translates the color of the hair as "ccrulei" and the eyes as "azzurri"; see his *Gli Apocrifi del Nuovo Testamento*, vol. 3, p. 138. Moraldi also rightly translates the Latin: "*I suoi capelli hanno il colore delle noci di Sorrento . . . I suoi occhi sono azzurri, vivaci e brillanti.*" Moraldi, *Apocrifi del Nuovo Testamento*, vol. 2, p. 1656.

21 See McClintock and Strong, *Cyclopedia*, vol. 5, p. 349.

22 For bibliographical information, see Charlesworth with Mueller, *The New Testament Apocrypha and Pseudepigrapha*, pp. 345–46.

23 See Charlesworth, *Jesus Within Judaism* (Anchor Bible Reference Library 1; New York: Doubleday, 1988) pp. 90–102 and J. P. Meier, *A Marginal Jew: Rethinking the Historical Jesus* (Anchor Bible Reference Library; New York: Doubleday, 1991) vol. 1, pp. 56–88.

24 See Charlesworth with Mueller, *The New Testament Apocrypha and Pseudepigrapha*, ad loc. cit.

25 For a recent discussion of this fact and for bibliographical assistance see R. Bizzocchi, *Chiesa e potere nella Toscana del Quattrocento* (Annali dell'Istituto storico italo-germanico Monografia 6; Bologna: Societa editrice il Mulino, 1987).

26 Dobschutz, *Christusbilder*, pp. 325–330.

27 Other documents, such as the *Sibylline Oracles*, the *Ascension of Isaiah*, the *Odes of Solomon*, the Christian preface and appendix to *Fourth Ezra*, the Christian portions of the *Testament of Adam*, and the *Apocalypse of Zachariah* need to be included, even though they are not pseudepigraphically attributed to a New Testament individual.

28 Also see Charlesworth, "Research on the New Testament Apocrypha and Pseudepigrapha," *Aufstieg und Niedergang der Romischen Welt* II. 25. 5, pp. 3919–68.

29 H. Koester, *Ancient Christian Gospels: Their History and Development* (Philadelphia: Trinity Press International, 1990).

30 The Synoptics are Matthew, Mark, and Luke. They are "synoptic" because they contain much of the same material and can be studied side-by-side.

31 See now G. J. Riley, *Resurrection Reconsidered: Thomas and John in Controversy* (Minneapolis: Fortress, 1995). Riley rightly sees how closely linked theologically and sociologically are the GosJn and the *GosTh*, but he judges the communities behind these gospels to be in competition. I am convinced he errs here, and one of the main reasons for this misperception is his misinterpretation of Thomas in the GosJn (see esp. his comments on p. 79).

32 See M. Hengel, *Die johanneische Frage* (WUNT 67; Tübingen: Mohr [Siebeck], 1993).

33 Q (an abbreviation for the German *Quelle*, meaning "source") is the name given by scholars to a presumed document which has not been found. Its existence is posited to explain the sayings of Jesus found in Matthew and Luke, but not in Mark.

34 The Diatessaron is a single gospel narrative compiled by Tatian around 170 CE. It is a combination of the canonical and also extra-canonical gospels—a "harmony" of the gospels. It was very popular for centuries. However, no manuscript of the original survives. We know it only through translations, commentaries, quotations of it in other works, and fragments of the original.

35 Valley Forge: Trinity Press International, 1995.

36 W. Schneemelcher, ed., English translation edited by R. McL. Wilson, *New Testament Apocrypha*, 2 vols. (Cambridge: James Clarke & Co. /Louisville: Westminster, 1991–1992 [revised edition]). Important for research is the original German: W. Schneemelcher, ed., *Neutestamentliche Apokryphen*, 2 vols. (Tübingen: Mohr [Siebeck], 1990 [vol. 1, 6th edition] 1989 [vol. 2, 5th edition]).

37 A codex is a manuscript with pages in book form, as opposed to a scroll which must be unrolled to access the material on it. The plural form is codices. Codex Sinaiticus is one of the oldest manuscripts of the Greek Bible. Dating to the fourth century, this work contains most of the OT, the NT, the *Epistle of Barnabas*, and the *Shepherd of Hermas*.

38 Syrus Sinaiticus is the copy of the Old Syriac Gospels preserved in a palimpsest manuscript in St. Catherine's Monastery in the Sinai desert [palimpsest means a document that contains at least two writings on top of each other. In antiquity an earlier writing was sometims scraped away and another penned over it; writing material was expensive and scarce].

39 The *Didache* (Greek for "Teaching") is an early Christian manual providing rules for conduct and discipline. Several slightly different versions have been preserved in part in other ancient writings and in a nearly complete manuscript dating to around 1000 CE, which was discovered in 1873. The *Didache* was probably composed sometime after 100 CE.

40 Oxyrhynchus was an Egyptian city of the Roman Period. It now lies under the modern town of Behnesa, about 125 miles south of Cairo. Grenfell and Hunt discovered four fragmentary papyrus texts there in a series of archaeological expeditions around the turn of the century. Three of these texts are collections of the sayings of Jesus. The fourth is a gospel. Eventually thousands of fragments were found at Oxyrhynchus. Papyri is the plural of papyrus, the material on which many ancient manuscripts were written.

41 J. K. Elliott, *The Apocryphal New Testament* (Oxford: At the Clarendon, 1993).

42 M. R. James, *The Apocryphal New Testament* (Oxford: At the Clarendon, 1924).

43 For example, in the *Letter of Lentulus*, which is straight out from James (with some changes in punctuation and style), we are told that Jesus is both "a man in stature middling tall," and "in stature of body tall . . . . " Jesus cannot be both of medium height and tall, and the error does not derive from the Latin. Jesus' eyes are also not "grey" (James and Elliott). The modern Italian translations are representative with suggesting an azure blue (see the previous section). Also, Elliott (p. 163) follows James (p. 151) in mistranslating the Coptic narrative of Jesus' passion; Jesus is not "reminding" Thomas "of the signs at the crucifixion" he is "showing" him these.

44 See Charlesworth and C. A. Evans, "Jesus in the Agrapha and Apocryphal Gospels," in *Studying the Historical Jesus: Evaluations of the State of Current Research*, ed. B. Chilton and Evans (New Testament Tools and Studies 19; Leiden, New York: Brill, 1994) pp. 478–533.

45 H. Merkel, "Appendix: the 'Secret Gospel' of Mark," *New Testament Apocrypha*, vol. 1, pp. 106–109.

46 Elliott, *The Apocryphal New Testament*, p. 148. The original is *"Die Entstehungszeit des 'geheimen Evangeliums' liegt wohl nicht vor der Mitte des 2. Jahrhunderts."* *Neutestamentliche Apokryphen*, vol. 1, p. 92.

47 See, as an example, Charlesworth, "Excluded Documents," in *The New Testament Apocrypha and Pseudepigrapha*, pp. 6–11.

48 Oddly it is now housed among the Old Testament Pseudepigrapha, although the contributors are convinced it is clearly a Christian composition. See Charlesworth, "Odes of Solomon," *The Old Testament Pseudepigrapha*, ed. Charlesworth (Garden City, N. Y. : Doubleday, 1985) vol. 2, pp. 725–71. J. A. Emerton, "The Odes of Solomon," *The Apocryphal Old Testament*, ed. H. F. D. Sparks (Oxford: At the Clarendon, 1984) pp. 683–731.

49 W. Bauer, "Die Oden Salomos," *Neutestamentliche Apokryphen in deutscher Übersetzung*, eds. E. Hennecke and W. Schneemelcher (Tubingen: Mohr [Siebeck], 1964 [3rd ed.]) vol. 2, pp. 576–625.

50 R. McL. Wilson, *The New Testament Apocrypha*, by E. Hennecke, ed. W. Schneemelcher, English edition ed. by R. McL. Wilson (London: Lutterworth/Philadelphia: Westminster, 1965) vol. 2, p. 12.

51 *Acts of Thomas* (in which the Hymn of the Pearl is now usually found) 109. 43–44, according to Elliott, *The Apocryphal New Testament*, p. 489.

52 See D. M. Smith, "The Problem of John and the Synoptics in Light of the Relation Between Apocryphal and Canonical Gospels," in *John and the Synoptics*, ed. A. Denaux (Leuven: Leuven University Press, 1992) pp. 147–62.

53 W. Bauer, *Rechtgläubigkeit und Ketzerei in ältesten Christentum* (BHT 10; Tübingen, 1934, 1964 [2nd edition with appendices by G. Strecker]); English translation (ET): *Orthodoxy and Heresy in Earliest Christianity*, trans. by a team and edited by R. A. Kraft and G. Krodel (Philadelphia: Fortress, 1971).

54 Nag Hammadi denotes an archaeological site near the village of al-Qasr in Egypt. In 1945, thirteen leather-bound books were found near Nag Hammadi under a boulder in a large jar. They were copied around 400 CE, making them among the oldest preserved codices. The books are written in Coptic, the native language of Egypt at that time. They contain Gnostic and Christian writings, translated from Greek or perhaps, in some cases, Syriac. The most well known of these is the *Gospel of Thomas*.

55 The hallmark of this phase is the publication of J. A. Fabricius's monumental *Codex Apocryphus Novi Testamenti* (2 vols., Hamburg, 1703, 1719).

56 Of the many hallmarks that could be listed for this period, only three will be mentioned briefly: J. -P. Migne's *Dictionnaire des Apocryphes, ou collection de tous les livres apocryphes* (2 vols., Paris, 1856–1858); K. Tischendorf's volumes—especially his *Acta Apostolorum Apocrypha* (Leipzig, 1851), *Apocalypses Apocryphae* (Leipzig, 1866), and *Evangelia Apocrypha* (Leipzig, 1876); and A. Resch's *Aussercanonische Paralleltexte zu den Evangelien* (4 vols. ; TU 10:1, 2, 3, 4; Leipzig, 1893 –96).

57 A. Harnack's *Lehrbuch der Dogmengeschichte* (3 vols., Tübingen, 1909) is an exemplary product of the nineteenth century each foreword is dated 1885, 1887, 1893, and 1909

58 The new tendency, foreshadowed in Resch's books, breaks into the open in four publications by B. P. Grenfell and A. S. Hunt, namely *Sayings of Our Lord from an Early Greek Papyrus* (London, 1897), *New Sayings of Jesus and Fragment of a Lost Gospel from Oxyrhynchus* (with L. W. Drexel, London, 1897, repr. 1904), *Fragment of an Uncanonical Gospel from Oxyrhynchus* (Oxford, 1908), and *The Oxyrhynchus Papyri* (6 vols., London, 1908).

59 The German title means "The Unknown Words of Jesus." Different editions were published in Zürich in 1948, 1951, and 1963. English translations were published in 1957 and 1964. Three other hallmarks of the third phase were W. Bauer's two masterpieces, *Das Leben Jesu im Zeitalter der Neutestamentlichen Apokryphen* (Tübingen, 1909, repr. 1967) and the paradigmatically important *Rechtgläubigkelt und Ketzerei im ältesten Christentum* (BHT 10; Tübingen, 1934, 1964 [2d. ed. with appendices by G. Strecker]; for ET see note 53 above), E. Hennecke's *Handbuch zu den Neutestamentlichen Apokryphen* (Tübingen, 1904) and *Neutestamentliche Apokryphen* (Tübingen, 1904, 1924; expanded to 2 vols. in 1959 and 1964 with W. Schneemelcher; and translated into English in 1963–1965), and finally M. R. James's *The Apocryphal New Testament* (Oxford, 1924, repr. 1926–1969). Hennecke's collection of the NTAP, as the successive editions and the English translation indicate, dominated the field; and the real interest was in volume one subtitled, *Gospels and Related Writings*.

60   H. Koester, *Introduction to the New Testament.*

61   L. E. Keck, "Is the New Testament a Field of Study? or, From Outler to Overbeck and Back," *Second Century* 1 (1981) 19–35.

62   C. W. Hedrick, for example, argues insightfully for the possible authenticity of numerous sayings about the Kingdom of Heaven in the gnostic *Apocryphon of James.* See his "Kingdom Sayings and Parables of Jesus in the Apocryphon of James: Tradition and Redaction," *NTS* 29 (1983) 1–21. S. L. Davies, however, tends to exaggerate the importance of the *Gospel of Thomas* for recovering Jesus' authentic words. He treats too cavalierly the possible gnostic focus of many of the sayings, and it is certainly inaccurate to report that scholars have concluded the *Gospel of Thomas* is gnostic because it was found among gnostic documents. As Charlesworth's *The New Testament Apocrypha and Pseudepigrapha* reveals, over 400 works have been published on this document. (J. H. Charlesworth, *The New Testament Apocrypha and Pseudepigrapha: A Guide to Publications, with Excursuses on Apocalypses*, ATLA Bibliography Series, no. 17: Metuchen, N. J. and London, 1987). Many of these conclude correctly that the present shape of this gospel is gnostic. Davies also confuses the facts when he claims that the *Gospel of Thomas* "may be our best source for Jesus' teachings. And then again, it may not be" (p. 9). See S. L. Davies, "Thomas: The Fourth Synoptic Gospel," *BA* 46 (1983) 6–9, 12–14. (Also see his "A Cycle of Jesus' Parables," *BA* 46 [1983] 15–17; and *The Gospel of Thomas and Christian Wisdom* [New York, 1983].)

63 In the new or fourth phase, we must single out the appearance of two impressive collections of the NTAP. In chronological order they are M. Erbetta's *Gli Apocrifi del Nuovo Testamento* (3 vols.—actually 4, vol. 1 is in two books, Turin, 1966–75) and L. Moraldi, *Apocrifi del Nuovo Testamento* (2 vols., Classici delle Religioni, sezione 5; Turin, 1971). Each of these is in the great tradition of Fabricius, Migne, James, and Hennecke-Schneemelcher-Wilson; moreover, they are informed and included documents most scholars have never read.

64 My translation from "Vers une nouvelle édition de la littérature apocrypha chrétienne: La Series Apocryphorum du Corpus Christianorum" (*Aug* 23 [1983] 373–78) 373.

65 My comments are not intended to be categorical. Many documents in the NTAP were considered 'gnostic' by the Church Fathers. The exact relationship between the documents in the NTAP and gnostic works is complex and deserves a separate full examination. A convenient English edition of the Nag Hammadi codices is published under the editorship of J. M. Robinson, *The Nag Hammadi Library in English* (New York, London, 1977). Also see the discussion of these apocalypses in my *The New Testament Apocrypha and Pseudepigrapha*, part III. R. H. Charles and W. O. E. Oesterly listed items in the NTAP writings that they admitted are "mainly gnostic"; this procedure would now add confusion. See their "Apocryphal Literature" *Encyclopaedia Britannica* (1956) vol. 2, pp. 105–108.

66 I include only documents heavily redacted by Christians, not those with single interpolations. For a distinction between redaction and interpolation, see J. H. Charlesworth, "Reflections on the SNTS Pseudepigrapha Seminar at Duke on the Testaments of the Twelve Patriarchs," *NTS* 23 (1977) 296–304.

67 See Charlesworth, *The New Testament Apocrypha and Pseudepigrapha*, category 19.

68 A. D. Nock, "The Gospels" *JTS* N. S. 11 (1960) 63–70.

69 Charlesworth, "Tatian's Dependence upon Apocryphal Traditions," *HeyJ* 15 (1974) 5–17.

70 E. J. Goodspeed, *Strange New Gospels*, (Chicago, 1931) pp. vii-viii.

71 See Goodspeed, *Strange New Gospels*, pp. 96–97. Also see Goodspeed's *Modern Apocrypha* (Boston, 1956) and his *Famous Hoaxes* (Grand Rapids, Mich., 1956).

72 P. Beskow has made the modern forgeries the subject of his *Strange Tales About Jesus: A Survey of Unfamiliar Gospels* (Philadelphia, 1983).

73 R. L. Anderson, "The Fraudulent Archko Volume," Brigham Young University Studies 15 (1974) 43–64.

74 Another hoax, probably plagiarized from *PsMt*, *InfGosTh*, and *Arabic InfGos*, is the Following: C. Mendès, *L'Évangile de la jeunesse de Notre-Seigneur Jésus-Christ d'après S. Pierre* (Paris, 1894; with Latin text and trans.); H. C. Greene, *The Gospel of the Childhood of Our Lord Jesus Christ* (London, 1904).

75 See S. Baring-Gould, *The Gospel of Judas, The Lost and Hostile Gospels* (London, 1874) pp. 299–305; A. de Santos Otero, "Judas," *Altslavischen Apok.*, vol. 2, pp. 119–28; F. A. Brunklaus, *Het Evangelie van Judas, Het Hooglied van Maria Magdalena, de Openbaring van de Apostel Thomas* (Maastricht, 1969); E. Amann, "Évangile de Judas," *DBSup* 1., col. 479; Fabricius, "Evangelium Judae Ischariothae," *Cod. Apoc. NT.*, 1, pp. 352–53; F. Repp, "Untersuchungen zu den Apokryphen der Österr. Nationalbibliothek: Die russische kirchenslavische Judas-Vita des Cod. Slav. 13," *Wiener Slavist. Jahrbuch* 7 (1957) 5–34.

76 Other works far too late for the NTAP, and perhaps Slavic compositions, are included in A. de Santos Otero's *Altslavischen Apok.*

77 See A. van Lantschoot, "Un texte palimpsest de Vat copte 65," *Muséon* 60 (1947) 261–68.

78 Two very different works receive the name *Gospel of Barnabas*. One is very early and was condemned by the Gelasian Decree. This pseudepigraphon is lost. Another *Gospel of Barnabas* appeared in Italian, but it dates from perhaps as late as the fifteenth century. For publications on this document, which is too late for inclusion in the NTAP (unless it proves to contain remnants of earlier works), see the following: S. Abdul-Ahad and W. H. Gairdner, *The Gospel of Barnabas: An Essay and Inquiry* (Hydrarabad, India, 1975); W. E. A. Axion, "On the Mohammedan Gospel of Barnabas" *JTS* 3 (1902) 441–451; O. Bardenhewer, "Der sog. Barnabasbrief," GAL,

vol. 1, pp. 103–16; H. Bergma, "Het 'Evangelie naar Barnabas,'"
in *Christusprediking in de wereld: Studien J. H. Bavinick* (Kampen,
1965); L. Cirillo, *L'Évangile de Barnabé*, 3 vols. (Paris, 1975); Idem,
Évangile de Barnabé: Recherches sur la composition et l'origine (Paris,
1977); Idem, "Le Pseudo-Clementine e il Vangelo di Barnaba della
Biblioteca nazionale di Vienna," *Asprenas* 18 (1971) 333–69; Idem,
"Un nuovo vangelo apocrifo: Il Vangelo di Barnaba," *Rivista di
Storia e Letteratura Religiosa* 11 (1975); 391–412; Idem, "Le sources
de l'Évangile de Barnabé," *RHR* 189 (1976): 130–35; Idem, "Le
'Vrais Pharisiens' dans l'Év. apocryphe de Barnabé," *RHR* 191
(1977) 121–28; Idem, and M. Frémaux, *Évangile de Barnabé* (Paris,
1977); H. Corbin, "Theologoumena Iranica" *Studia Iranica* 5
(1976) 225–35; F. P. Cotterell, "The Gospel of Barnabas," *Vox
Evangelica* 10 (1977) 43–47; M. de Epalza, "Sobre un posible autor
español del 'Evangelio de Barnabé,'" *Al-Andalus* 28 (1963) 479–91;
M. Erbetta, "Vangelo di Barnaba," *Apoc. Del NT*, 1. 2, pp. 225–26;
J. E. Fletcher, "The Spanish Gospel of Barnabas," *NovT* 18 (1976)
314–20; G. Jeffery, *The Gospel According to Barnabas* (London,
1975); J. Jomier, "Une énigme persistante: L'Évangile dit de
Barnabé," *Mélanges de l'Institute Dominican d'Études Orientales* 14
(1980) 271–300; Idem, "L'Évangile selon Barnabé," *Mélanges de
l'Instituti Dominicin d'Études Orientales* 6 (1959–61) 137–226; M. F.
Kermani, *Enjil-e Barnābā* (Teheran, 1968); J. M. Magnin, "En
Marge de l'ébionisme: L'Évangile de Barnabé," *Proche-orient
chrétien* 29 (1979) 44–64; M. Philoneko, "Une tradition essénienne
dans l'Évangile de Barnabas," *Mélanges d'historie des religions offerts à
Henri-Charles Puech*, eds. P. Lévy and E. Wolff (Paris, 1974) pp.
191–95; L. Ragg, *The Gospel of Barnabas* (Oxford, 1907); Idem,
"The Mohammedan 'Gospel of Barnabas'," *JTS* 6 (1905) 424–33;
A. D. Santos Otero, "Evangelio de Barnabé (el Italiano),"
Evangelios Apócrifos, pp. 24–25; J. Slomp, "The Pseudo-Gospel of
Barnabas: Muslim and Christian Evaluations," *Al-Mushir* 18
(1976). N. V.; Stegmüller, *Repertorium Biblicum*, vol. 1, p. 108, vol.
8, pp. 80–81; R. Stichel, "Bemerkungen zum
Barnabas-Evangelium," *Byzantino-Slavica* 43 (1982) 189–201; H.
Suasso, "Some Remarks on the 'Gospel of Barnabas'" [in
Indonesian], *Orientasi* 3 (1971) 78–86; R. McL. Wilson, "Barnabas,
Gospel of," *ZPEB*, vol. 1, p. 479.

79 See Minge, *Dictionnaire*, 2, cols. 953–54.

80 See Minge, *Dictionnaire*, 2, cols. 959–60.

81 See Fabricius, "Evangelium Aeternum," *Cod. Apoc. NT*, 1, pp. 337–38.

82 This document on the mother of "the Virgin" is actually a legend and not an apocryphon, but those two categories considerably overlap. It seems too late for inclusion in the NTAP. See Minge, *Dictionnaire*, 2, cols. 105–106; also see Migne, *Dictionnaire des légendes du Christianisme* (Paris 1855) col. 1220; and P. V. Charland, *Les trois légendes de madame sainte Anne* (Montreal, 1898).

83 See Migne, *Dictionnaire*, 2, col. 112.

84 P. Pratten, "The Teaching of Simon Cephas in the City of Rome," ANF 8, pp. 673–75; W. Cureton, ed., "Acts of Simon-Kepha in the City of Rome" *Ancient Syriac Documents Relative to the Earliest Establishment of Christianity in Edessa and the Neighboring Countries* (London, 1864) pp. 35–41.

85 Charlesworth, *The New Testament Apocrypha and Pseudepigrapha*, pp. 309–14.

86 See especially the introduction, Greek texts and English translation by R. P. Casey and R. W. Thompson, titled, "A Dialogue Between Christ and the Devil," *JTS* N.S. 6 (1955) 49–65. Also see, in chronological order, the following erudite publications: A. N. Pypin, *False and Dismissed Books* (Moscow [?], 1862) pp. 86–88 [Russian]; N. S. Tikhonravov, *Monuments of Dismissed Russian Literature* (Moscow, 1863) pp. 282–288 [Russian]; A. Vassilev, *Anecdota greaco-byzantina* (Moscow, 1893) pp. 4–10; S. Novaković, "Apocrif o prepiranju Isusa Hrista sa djavolom" *Starine* 16 (1884) 86–89; G. Polívka, "Opsi i izvodi??," *Starine* 21 (1889) 200–203; N. Bonwetsch, in: *Harnack, Gesch. Altchrist. Lit.* (1893) vol. 2, p. 910; K. F. Radčenko, *Zametki o pergamennon* (Moscow [?], 1903) pp. 175–211; K. F. Radčenko, *Etjudy po bogomil'stvu, Izbornik Kievskij v čest*, T. D. Florinskogo (Kiev, 1904) pp. 28–38; R. Strohal, *State hrvatske apokrifine* (Bjelovar, 1917) pp. 54–56; J. Ivanov, *Bogomilski knigi i legendi* (Sofia, 1925) pp. 248–57; É. Turndeanu, "Apocryphes bogomiles et apocryphes pseudobogomiles," *RHR* 138 (1950) 194–97; A. de Santos Otero, "Diaboli cum Jesu Contentio," *Altslavischen Apok.*, 2, pp. 156–60.

87 This so-called "apocalypse" is lost; it probably was not an apocalypse. See my comments in "Documents Often Considered to

Be 'Apocalypses,'" in *The New Testament Apocrypha and Pseudepigrapha*, pp. 57–58.

88 For this Irish apocryphon, see the impressive and learned work by M. McNamara titled *The Apocrypha in the Irish Church* (Dublin Institute for Advanced Studies; Dublin, 1975) pp. 115–118, 132. McNamara, in his discussion of *Tenga Bithnua* (The Ever New Tongue), refers to the possibility that the "Apocalypse of Philip" was used by the redactor of the Irish work, but wisely states that it "is difficult to determine what sources the author used (p. 115)." Also see M. Erbetta, "Apocrifi Irlandesi (Medioevo)," *Apoc del. NT.*, 3, p. 483.

89 A full list of excluded works would move our whole discussion of the NTAP off center and into medieval and even later literature. Many writings with titles similar to those of documents in the NTAP are simply medieval compositions. For example, the *Epistle Concerning the Life and Passion of Our Lord Jesus Christ* is far too late for the NTAP. See M. Hedlund, *Epistola de Vita et Passione Domini Nostri: Der Lateinische Text mit Einleitung und Kommentar* (Kerkhistorische Bijdragen; Leiden, 1975).

90 Koester informed me that a second edition of the English translation of volume one appeared in 1995; it was published by Walter de Gruyter in Berlin. The English edition of volume two is slated for 1998.

91 Until the winter of 1886–87 the *Gospel of Peter* was known only through one clear reference: Eusebius' *H. E.* 6. 12. 2–6.

92 A. Harnack, *Bruchstücke des Evangeliums und der Apokalypse des Petrus* (TU 9; Leipzig, 1893). A. Harnack, and H. V. Schubert, "Das Petrusevangelium," *TLZ* 19 (1894) 9–18.

93 T. Zahn, *Das Evangelium des Petrus* (Erlangen, Leipzig, 1893).

94 R. Cameron, *The Other Gospels: Non-Cannonical Gospel Texts* (Philadelphia, 1982).

95 Koester, "History and Development of Mark's Gospel (From Mark to Secret Mark and 'Cannonical' Mark)," in *Colloquy on New Testament Studies: A Time for Reappraisal and Fresh Approaches*, B. Corley, ed. (Macon, Georgia, 1983) pp. 35–57.

96 J. D. Crossan, *Four Other Gospels: Shadows on the Contours of Canon* (Minneapolis, Chicago, and New York, 1985) p. 133.

97   The chapters were added by J. A. Robinson. See his *The Gospel According to Peter,* and the *Revelation of Peter* (London, 1892). Independently, verses which run consecutively throughout the document were supplied by A. Harnack. See note 91. The text is that published by U. Bouriant "Fragments du livre d'Enoch et de quelques écrits attribués à saint Pierre," *Mémoires publiées par les membres de la Mission archéologique française au Caire* 9.1 (Paris, 1892) pp. 137–142. It was republished by A. de Santos in *Los Evangelos Apócrifos* (Madrid, 1956, 1975 [3rd ed.]). The Greek is also published by Charlesworth in *ANRW* II 25.5 (1988) 3936-3938.

98   N. B. Tatro (AP), "Love Letter Found Among Scrolls—Scholar: Note May Be From Samson to Delilah," The News Herald (Panama City) June, 30, 1990. The reporter did not grasp that he had been listening to a joke.

About the Author

James H. Charlesworth received an A.B. from Ohio Wesleyan University, a B.D. from Duke Divinity School, a Ph.D. from Duke Graduate School, and an advanced degree from the École Biblique de Jérusalem. He has been on the faculty of Duke University, the Universität Tübingen, and The Hebrew University, Jerusalem, Israel. Since 1984, he has been the George L. Collord Professor of New Testament Language and Literature at Princeton Theological Seminary. He has written or edited more than thirty books and 200 articles, including editing of the first comprehensive English language edition of the Pseudepigrapha. Some of his recent books include *Jesus Within Judaism* (Doubleday), *Jesus' Jewishness* (Crossroad), *What Has Archaeology to Do with Faith* (Trinity), *The Messiah* (Fortress), *Jesus and the Dead Sea Scrolls* (Doubleday), *Qumran Questions* (Sheffield) and *The Beloved Disciple*. He has been involved in the discovery of more than four thousand biblical and religious manuscripts and has worked on photographing and translating the Dead Sea Scrolls. He is the editor of BIBAL's Dead Sea Scrolls & Christian Origins Library and the editor of the Dead Sea Scrolls Project at Princeton Theological Seminary.

The Dead Sea Scrolls & Christian Origins Library

Vol. 1 (April 1998) The Destruction of Jerusalem, Joseph Peeples.
ISBN 0-941037-62-2

Vol. 3 (Feb. 1998) How Barisat Bellowed: Folklore, Humor, and
Iconography in the Jewish Apocalypses and the Apocalypse
of John, James Charlesworth. **ISBN 0-941037-64-9**

Vol. 4 (Jun 1998) Early Christologies: New Insights in Light of the
DSS and the Nag Hammadi Codices, Petr Pokorný.
ISBN 0-941037-65-7

Subsequent Volumes (order of publication not yet determined)
By James Charlesworth—
  Another Davidson Affair: The Son of David is Solomon
  The Apocalypse of John: Its Theology and Influence on Christian
    Apocrypha
  Fearless Awe: The Christology of Awe
  The Foreground of the Background: Jewish Messianism and the
    Origins of Christianity
  Light Over Darkness: The Fourth Gospel and DSS
  Loving the Beloved: The Spirituality of the Odes of Solomon
  A Missing Link in Christian Theology: Christian Origins & the DSS
  Moving Semitic Prose: Jesus and His Contemporary, Hillel
  Much Water There: John the Baptizer and the DSS
  Spirituality Matters: The Theology of the DSS
By Philip Alexander—Hillel, The Teacher of Righteousness
By Rami Arav—Bethsaida and Biblical Archaeology
By Magen Broshi—The Archaeology of the DSS
By Joseph Dan—The Origin of Jewish Mysticism
By Michal Dayagi-Mendels—Biblical Archaeology: An Introduction
By Karl Donfried—Paul and the DSS
By Isaiah Gafni—The Symbolism of the Land
By John R. Levison—The Spirit in Second Temple Judaism: Seers,
  Saints, and Scholars
By James Strange—Sepphoris and the Palestinian Jesus Movement
By James Tabor—Last Days in Jerusalem: Ancient Jews and
  Christians at the Crossroad
By Shemaryahu Talmon—The Importance of the Qumran
  Calendar

(Titles subject to change)

Call **1-888-788-2280** to order.